Memory
Current Issues
SECOND EDITION

Gillian Cohen
George Kiss
and
Martin Le Voi

Open University Press
Buckingham · Philadelphia

Open University Press
Celtic Court
22 Ballmoor
Buckingham
MK18 1XW

and
1900 Frost Road, Suite 101
Bristol, PA 19007, USA

In association with The Open University

First published 1986 as *Memory: A Cognitive Approach*.
Second edition first published 1993
Reprinted in this edition 1993, 1994, 1995, 1996

ISBN 0 335 19079 0

A CIP catalogue record for this book is available from the British Library

Library of Congress Cataloging-in-Publication Data is available

Edited and designed by The Open University
Typeset by Graphicraft Typesetters Limited, Hong Kong
Printed in Great Britain by Biddles Limited, Guildford and King's Lynn

Memory
Current Issues
SECOND EDITION

Open Guides to Psychology

Series Editor: Judith Greene, Professor of Psychology at the Open University

Titles in the series

Learning to Use Statistical Tests in Psychology
Judith Greene and Manuela D'Oliveira

Basic Cognitive Processes
Judith Greene and Carolyn Hicks

Memory: Current Issues (Second Edition)
Gillian Cohen, George Kiss and Martin Le Voi

Language Understanding: A Cognitive Approach
Judith Greene

Problem Solving: Current Issues (Second Edition)
Hank Kahney

Perception and Representation
Ilona Roth and John Frisby

Designing and Reporting Experiments
Peter Harris

Biological Foundations of Behaviour
Frederick Toates

Running Applied Psychology Experiments
John Leach

Memory

Contents

Part I Everyday Memory

Gillian Cohen

Part IIA Memory Systems: The Experimental Approach

Gillian Cohen (based on an earlier version by Michael W. Eysenck)

Part IIB Memory Systems: The Computer Modelling Approach

George Kiss

Part III Parallel Distributed Processing and Its Application in Models of Memory
Martin Le Voi

Overview

Martin Le Voi

Preface

Within the Open Guides to Psychology series, *Memory* is one of a companion set of four books, the others being *Language Understanding*, *Problem Solving* and *Perception and Representation*. Together these form the main texts of the Open University third level course in Cognitive Psychology, but each of the four volumes can be read independently. The course is designed for second or third year students. It is presented in the style and format that the Open University has found to be uniquely effective in making the material intelligible and interesting.

The books provide an up-to-date, in-depth treatment of some of the major issues, theories and findings in cognitive psychology. They are designed to introduce a representative selection of different research methods, and the reader is encouraged, by means of Activities and Self-assessment Questions interpolated through the text, to become involved in cognitive psychology as an active participant.

The authors gratefully acknowledge the many helpful comments and suggestions of fellow members of the course team and of the external assessor Michael W. Eysenck on earlier drafts, and the valuable assistance of Pat Vasiliou in typing the manuscript.

Acknowledgements

Grateful acknowledgement is made to Michael W. Eysenck. Part IIA is based on the version he wrote for a previous edition of this book. Thanks also to John Slack and Hank Kahney who wrote material upon which Part IIB is partly based.

Grateful acknowledgement is also made to the following sources for permission to reproduce material in this book:

Figures

Figures 1.2 and 1.3: Lachman, J.L., Lachman, R. and Thronesberry, C. (1979) 'Metamemory through the adult life span', *Developmental Psychology*, 15, pp. 543–51, copyright © 1979 by the American Psychological Association, adapted by permission; *Figure 1.7*: Neisser, U. (1982) *Memory Observed: Transformations of Memory in Everyday Life*, W.H. Freeman and Co.; *Figure 1.8*: adapted from Holding, D.H., Noonan, T.K., Pfau, H.D. and Holding, C.S. (1986) 'Date attribution, age and the distribution of life memories', *Journal of Gerontology*, 41, pp. 481–5, copyright © The Gerontological Society of America; *Figure 2.3*: Wilding, J. and Mohindra, D. (1980) 'Effects of subvocal suppression, articulating aloud and noise on sequence', *British Journal of Psychology*, 71, pp. 247–61, British Psychological Society; *Figure 2.4*: Hitch, G. and Baddeley, A.D. (1976) 'Verbal reasoning and working memory', *Quarterly Journal of Experimental Psychology*, 28, pp. 603–21, Lawrence Erlbaum Associates, copyright © The Experimental Psychology Society; *Figures 2.5, 2.6, 2.7 and 2.8*: reprinted by permission of the publishers from *The Architecture of Cognition* by John R. Anderson, Cambridge, Mass.: Harvard University Press, copyright © 1983 by the President and Fellows of Harvard College; *Figure 3.1*: Anderson, J.A., Silverstein, J.W., Ritz, S.A. and Jones, R.S.L. (1977) 'Distinctive features, categorical perception and probability learning: some applications of a neural model', *Psychological Review*, 84, pp. 413–51, copyright 1977 by the American Psychological Association, adapted by permission; *Figures 3.8, 3.9, 3.10a–e and 3.11*: Rumelhart, D.E., Smolensky, P., McClelland, J.L. and Hinton, G.E. (1986) *Parallel Distributed Processing: Explorations in the Microstructure of Cognition*, Vol. 2, MIT Press; *Figures 3.12 and 3.13*: Seidenberg, M.S. and McClelland, J.L. (1989) 'A distributed, developmental model of word recognition and naming', *Psychological Review*, 96, pp. 523–68, copyright © 1989 by the American Psychological Association; *Figure 3.14*: Waters, G.S. and Seidenberg, M.S. (1985) 'Spelling-sound effects in reading: time course and decision criteria', *Memory and Cognition*, 13, pp. 557–72, Psychonomic Society Inc.; *Figure 3.15*: Brown, G.D.A. (1987) 'Resolving inconsistency: a computational model of word naming', *Journal of Memory and Language*, 26, pp. 1–2, Academic Press Inc.

Tables

Tables 3.5, 3.6, 3.7 and 3.8: adapted from Rumelhart, D.E., Smolensky, P., McClelland, J.L. and Hinton, G.E. (1986) *Parallel Distributed Processing: Explorations in the Microstructure of Cognition*, Vol. 2, MIT Press.

Introduction

This book is divided into three parts, each dealing with a different aspect of memory. Part I *Everyday Memory* is concerned with the way memory functions in everyday life. The reader will be on familiar ground here because everybody has first-hand experience of the way his or her own memory works in similar circumstances. The research discussed in this part focuses primarily on the contents of everyday memory, on what we remember and what we forget. While some things are remembered accurately, a great deal of what we experience in daily life is forgotten or misremembered. Several theories that have been proposed to explain the selective nature of everyday memory are outlined and discussed.

Parts II and III are concerned with the processes and mechanisms of memory. Part IIA *Memory Systems: The Experimental Approach* is concerned with the processing activities that occur in working memory when memories are input to the system. The theoretical construct of working memory corresponds to short-term memory but emphasizes the idea that information in working memory may be manipulated, transformed or utilized in ongoing cognitive tasks like talking and reading, doing mental arithmetic, or reasoning. Working memory is not just a receptacle in which information is temporarily dumped.

Part IIB *Memory Systems: The Computer Modelling Approach* takes a much broader theoretical view of memory as part of a larger cognitive system. It is less concerned with the fine details of the characteristics of human memory, but rather concentrates on the position and function of memory in the whole of human cognition. It is an attempt to integrate memory in a much wider theoretical structure. Nevertheless, the model discussed has obvious connections with the content of the previous sections, especially with regard to working memory (described in Part IIA) and schema theories (described in Part I).

Part III looks at an area of rising interest in psychology, that of parallel distributed processing (PDP). Often referred to as 'neural networks' (though the only true neural network is the living brain), these are causing some excitement amongst psychologists because of their capability of emulating some low-level characteristics of memory using very simple computational devices acting together. This Part concentrates on explaining what PDP models are and how they work (they are particularly good at learning for themselves) and ends by introducing some of the more controversial aspects of the scope of PDP models.

This book does not cover every aspect of human memory. Because all higher mental processes rely on memory, memory is involved in every area of cognitive psychology. In consequence, all the Cognitive Psychology volumes in the Open Guides to Psychology series cannot help but discuss the role of memory. One important issue in the study of memory concerns the way information is represented. Just as a given piece of information might be represented externally in sentences, in a table of numbers, in a graph, a picture or a diagram, so there are a variety of different forms that an internalized mental representation might take. Different kinds of memory representations underlie different cognitive activities, such as perception, language, and problem solving; these aspects of the memory system are considered separately in the three companion volumes to this Open Guide.

How to use this guide

In each part of the book the reader will find Activities and Self-Assessment Questions (SAQs) inserted at various points in the text. Doing the Activities will give a deeper insight and a better understanding of how some of the research techniques work. The SAQs provide the reader with a means of checking his or her understanding. The answers can be found at the end of the book and will help illuminate points made in the text.

Doing the Activities and answering the SAQs engages the reader as an active participant instead of just a passive recipient. He or she is forced to carry out the more active processing which is known to produce better comprehension and retention of what is read.

Detailed accounts of experiments are presented in Techniques Boxes and these are chosen as illustrative of representative experimental methods. The Summaries recapitulate the main points in each section and provide a useful aid to revision. The Index of Concepts that appears at the end of the book allows the reader to locate the place in the text where a concept is first introduced and defined. Entries in the Index of Concepts are italicized in the text.

Each part concludes with a short list of recommended further reading. Obviously the interested reader can also follow up the references given in the text. Some of these references are to *Cognitive Psychology: A Student's Handbook* by Eysenck and Keane, which is the set book for the Open University course in Cognitive Psychology.

Part I
Everyday Memory

Gillian Cohen

Contents

1   Introduction: the hundred years of silence

Psychologists have been studying memory for a hundred years. What is there to show for it? Many fascinating questions are thrown up by our day-to-day experience of the way our memories seem to work. Do old people really remember the distant past better than the recent past? Why do people who share exactly the same experience remember it differently? Why are certain episodes in our lives remembered in vivid detail when so much else seems to be lost without a trace? What do people remember of the subjects they studied at school? Why do we remember so little from the first years of our lives? You might think that all these puzzles would have been solved long ago but this is not so.

In 1978 Ulric Neisser drew attention to the 'thundering silence' with which psychologists responded when confronted with questions like these. The past hundred years had been spent in the laboratory concentrating almost entirely on theoretical questions about the underlying mechanisms of memory. Ordinary practical questions about how memory functions in daily life in the real world had not been considered important. One of the few exceptions is the work of Bartlett (1932). He did study memory for realistic material like stories, faces and pictures, but his ideas did not have much influence at that time.

Although laboratory experiments do not always shed light on remembering and forgetting in the world outside, working in laboratory conditions has many obvious advantages. It allows the experimenter to control rigorously the nature of the to-be-remembered material, the duration and timing of the presentation, the test environment, the instructions to the subject, the conditions under which the task is carried out, and so on. Techniques Box A shows a typical experiment of this kind, in which these factors are carefully regulated and standardized.

TECHNIQUES BOX A

Peterson and Peterson's Trigram Retention Experiment (1959)

Rationale
Peterson and Peterson wanted to study the rate of 'pure' short-term forgetting when no rehearsal is allowed.

Method
Their stimuli consisted of three consonants (called a trigram), which had to be recalled after an interval varying from 3 to 18 seconds

---

during which time subjects did an interpolated task to prevent them rehearsing. The experiment consisted of many trials, each consisting of the following sequence:

1 A trigram (e.g. XPJ) was presented acoustically (i.e. read out aloud).
2 A three-digit number was presented acoustically (e.g. 'four hundred and thirty six').
3 Subjects counted backwards aloud in threes (e.g. 436, 433, 430, 427, 424, etc.). This is the interpolated task which prevents rehearsal of the trigram.
4 Subjects continued to count for either 3, 6, 9, 12, 15 or 18 seconds, at the end of which time a tone signal was heard.
5 At the tone signal, subjects stopped counting backwards, and attempted to recall the trigram.

Results
Peterson and Peterson scored the subjects' recall, marking letters correct only when they were reported in the same place in the sequence as in the original. For example, if a subject recalled 'XJP' for 'XPJ', he or she was scored as recalling only one correct item. The results are shown in Figure 1.1. The average percentage correct recall of trigrams is high with short delays, but falls as the delay period increases. After 18 seconds of delay, subjects were correctly recalling only just over 10 per cent of the trigrams.

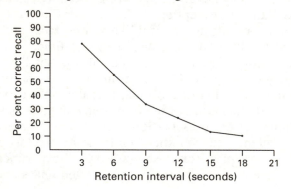

Figure 1.1   The percentage of trigrams correctly recalled, as a function of delay before recall (Peterson and Peterson, 1959)

The fact that most material in short-term memory (STM) is forgotten within a period of 6–12 seconds if it is not rehearsed was interpreted by Peterson and Peterson as evidence of the rate of decay of a short-term memory trace.

The results of laboratory experiments like this one are important for constructing and testing theoretical models of memory and for establishing parameters of the memory mechanism such as the rate of decay for items in short-term memory. Even so, studying memory in the laboratory is very different from studying memory in real life.

Think about the kind of things you have to remember on a typical day. These might include a shopping list, a recipe, telephoning a relative, filling the car up with petrol, the arguments put forward at a meeting, and the plot of a television play. The things we have to remember in the world outside the laboratory are not isolated lists of meaningless items. They include complex experiences in the past, plans for the future, facts and scenes embedded in a rich context of ongoing events and surrounding objects. When we encounter the stuff of real-life memories we are often inattentive, distracted or confused. Such memories may be recalled repeatedly, or may lie dormant for many years. Because the workings of everyday memory are so complicated and confused, there are many factors that cannot be measured or controlled and observations are often imprecise.

Since 1978 the hundred years of silence have come to an end. Psychologists have responded to Neisser's challenge and work on everyday memory is booming. This new wave of interest in the practical applied aspects of cognitive psychology is not confined to the study of memory. Vigorous efforts are under way to relate many areas of psychology to the mental activities of ordinary people going about their daily lives. Problems such as how doctors decide on a medical diagnosis, the reliability of witnesses in courts, the perceptual processes that underlie face recognition, and the skills involved in holding conversations, scheduling jobs to be done and planning routes are all being studied. This kind of research has what Neisser termed *ecological validity*. This means that it is based on real situations in real environments, and the findings arising from it have real applications. Neisser has been a strong advocate of ecological validity, and many psychologists engaged in the study of thinking have followed his lead.

However, some memory researchers (e.g. Banaji and Crowder, 1989) have argued that the pursuit of ecological validity is misguided. In their paper 'The bankruptcy of everyday memory'. Banaji and Crowder argue that studies which are high in ecological validity are necessarily low in generalizability. By this they mean that the results are specific to the particular situation and the particular people who were studied and cannot be generalized to other situations. So, according to this view, a study of how well people could recall the details of a traffic accident they witnessed only tells us how *those* people remembered *that* particular accident. The absence of any controls over what they actually saw, how much attention they were paying and how often they thought about it subsequently means that the study fails to yield any general principles about memory for events. Many psychologists remain unconvinced by Banaji and Crowder's arguments and believe that everyday memory research can be useful and valid if it is carefully designed. Ideally, traditional laboratory experiments and the everyday approach should be complementary. We need the theoretical framework derived from more rigorous experimental studies in order to interpret everyday memory phenomena and to try to draw some general conclusions about them. And, if theorizing is not to be sterile, it needs to be applied to the world outside the laboratory.

1.1   Methods for studying everyday memory

Researchers engaged in the realistic study of memory cannot just go about making observations of naturally occurring memory activities. To be informative, any research, even naturalistic research, must be guided by specific questions. The researcher must narrow the scope of enquiry so as to focus on some particular aspects of memory, and must devise some methods of testing or measuring how well memory works.

Two main approaches have been adopted. The first relies on *self-reports* or introspections, recording people's own observations about the way their memories function, about the things they remember and the things they forget. The second approach retains the methods of formal experimentation, but attempts to devise *naturalistic experiments* which are much more representative of real life. This usually involves asking people to remember natural material such as stories, films, events, or maps, instead of the traditional lists of letters, words or digits. In Part I of this volume we shall examine some examples of both kinds of research into everyday memory.

The use of self-reports by present-day psychologists is something of a turn around. Early psychologists like Wundt and Freud relied heavily on introspections as evidence for their theories, but self-reports were discredited during the Behaviourist era (roughly from the 1920s to the 1950s), when interest was focused on overt behaviour and the importance, and even existence, of mental events were discounted. Now psychologists who study thinking have begun to turn back the clock and the old *introspective methods* have been cautiously resurrected and brought back into use.

It is recognized that many of the very rapid mental processes that underlie activities like perceiving a complex scene, recognizing a word, or speaking a grammatical sentence, are simply not accessible to consciousness. In these cases, we are aware of the end product of the mental operations but not of the processes themselves. People cannot introspect and make verbal reports about what is going on in their heads below the level of consciousness, and we must accept that a lot of mental activity is unconscious. Nevertheless, there are some thought processes that do take place consciously and with some effort and practice people can become quite good at describing them. This is particularly true of so-called 'slow processes' — long drawn out mental processes like the strategies involved in solving problems, or attempts to reconstruct a memory from the past. There are many aspects of the mental processes underlying behaviour which are known to the actor but which are not necessarily apparent to an outside observer unless they are revealed by introspective report. These include plans and intentions, current sensations and emotions, past history, beliefs and judgements, reasons and motives. Introspective reports can, therefore, greatly enrich the researcher's understanding of the observed behaviour.

No method of psychological investigation is entirely foolproof and watertight. Self-reports may be unreliable if people exaggerate or distort them. People may not like to reveal the confused and muddled state of their mental processes, and may tidy up the reported version so as to seem more impressive. It is up to the researcher to guard against this and persuade subjects to be as accurate as possible. A more detailed discussion of the validity of introspective reports as evidence of mental processes can be found in Miller (1956) and in White (1988).

SAQ 1
Which of the following mental operations do you think would be 'accessible to introspection' so that someone could describe the mental processes involved? Which would be inaccessible to introspection? Why?
(a) Dividing 246 by 3.
(b) Considering a move at chess or draughts.
(c) Writing your own name.
(d) Recognizing a tune.
(e) Solving a crossword puzzle clue.

Naturalistic experiments also have some pitfalls. An experimental situation is never exactly representative of real life. Experimental subjects may be anxious about their performance when they know they will be tested; the task may seem pointless or boring, and the material, however realistic, is likely to be more simplified and orderly than real events. Psychologists who opt to study everyday memory have to accept these limitations, but are compensated by the relevance and interest of their findings.

Summary of Section 1

- Traditional laboratory experiments on memory are theoretically important but are too artificial to tell us much about memory in everyday life. These experiments are concerned with the *mechanisms* of memory rather than the *contents* of memory.
- A new wave of interest in everyday memory has sparked off studies which examine the working of memory in real-life situations. These

are primarily concerned with memory contents — with what is remembered and what is forgotten. Everyday memory research has ecological validity, but it is difficult to draw general conclusions unless some controls are imposed.

- The methods used to study everyday memory include asking people to describe the working of their own memories (introspective self-reports); and designing naturalistic experiments which try to mimic real-life situations as far as possible.

2 Metamemory

Metamemory means knowing what you know, knowing how your memory works, and being able to assess your own memory.

2.1 Self-rating questionnaires

One way in which self-report methods have been employed is by using questionnaires to find out about the kinds of memory abilities used in everyday life. Typically these questionnaires ask people how well they remember various kinds of things, or how often they forget others. Here are some examples of the kinds of questions that are asked. The respondent is asked to rate the frequency of forgetting and to circle the appropriate value. These values are known as *self-ratings*.

	Very often	Quite often	Occasionally	Very rarely	Never
How often do you forget appointments?	4	3	2	1	0
How often do you want to tell a joke but find you cannot remember it?	4	3	2	1	0
How often do you forget people's names?	4	3	2	1	0
When you go shopping, how often do you forget items you intended to buy?	4	3	2	1	0
How often do you forget the route to a particular place?	4	3	2	1	0

It is important to be quite clear about what this sort of questionnaire is actually measuring. The rating values obtained do not necessarily reflect memory ability; they reflect *beliefs about* memory ability. If the respondents are honest and accurate, these beliefs may correspond with actual memory ability. But can people assess their own memory efficiency accurately? They may be overboastful or overmodest. Even more worryingly, they may fail to remember how often they forget.

Self-ratings have proved to have high reliability. That is, if subjects are asked to complete a questionnaire and then, after an interval, it is administered again, there is a good agreement between the original and the repeated versions. However, some researchers consider that self-ratings obtained from these questionnaires are invalid (i.e. not a true measure of ability) because they do not correlate highly with scores obtained on objective tests of memory ability. Someone who gives good self-ratings on the questionnaire may have poor scores in an experimental test like recalling lists of words. But self-assessment methods are not necessarily discredited by this. The questionnaire and the experimental test are measuring different things, and there is really no reason why a person's score in a word list learning experiment should be considered a more valid reflection of his or her memory ability than the same person's own self ratings. Of course, test scores are more rigorous and more objective, but self-assessments are based on people's own first-hand experience of success and failure in a wide range of everyday tasks over a long period.

Some researchers (e.g. Broadbent *et al.*, 1982) have tried to check the validity of self-assessment by having a partner or close relative provide a parallel set of ratings. After all, your partner is probably well placed to give an objective opinion on how often you lose your car keys or forget the shopping. In fact, self-ratings have been found to correlate well with assessments made by a partner or relative. We can be reasonably confident that properly designed questionnaires provide fairly accurate information. They also reveal clearly that memory is not just 'good' or 'bad' overall. A person's memory has strengths and weaknesses. Some people are good at remembering some kinds of things and poor at others; other people have a different pattern of success and failure. The fact that memory seems, on this evidence, to consist of specific abilities, rather than a single unitary ability, fits in with current theoretical models in which memory is divided in to separate component sub-systems (see Part IIA, Sections 1 and 2).

Another advantage of questionnaires is that they can be used to explore not only differences between individuals but also differences between groups. The effects of brain injury, age-related changes and sex differences can be studied by analysing the responses of different groups. For example, in a study by Cohen and Faulkner (1984), elderly people rated themselves better than young people at remembering appointments but poorer at remembering names. Sunderland, Harris and Baddeley (1983) found that people who had suffered head injuries reported more difficulty in recognizing faces and in remembering stories than normal controls.

Activity
Answer the self-rating questions on page 20 to assess your own memory. Jot down the rating values you would give yourself for each question on a piece of paper. Then show the questionnaire to a partner/relative/ close friend/colleague and ask him or her to assess *your* memory, circling the appropriate rating values. Now cross-check the two assessments and see how well they agree. If they differ, try to work out why this might be.

2.2   *Knowing what you know*

By and large, most people know what they do know and what they don't know. This may seem obvious, but is in fact one of the most remarkable features of the human cognitive system. Given the enormous range and quantity of information that an adult accumulates and stores over a lifetime, it is surprising that when we are asked a question we can usually say with reasonable confidence whether the answer is in store or not. This ability is also demonstrated in lexical decision experiments when subjects have to decide whether a letter string is a real word or not. We are able to decide that a string like 'brone' is not a word so rapidly that it is clear we cannot have searched through the entire mental lexicon of around 60,000 words. Yet we know that 'brone' is not represented there. Paradoxically, we know whether the search will be successful *before* it has begun.

Often, however, it turns out that there are not just two alternatives — either giving the correct answer or not knowing. There is a *gradient of knowing*. This is nicely exemplified in the TV programme *Mastermind*, in which several kinds of permitted response reflect this gradient of knowing. Suppose, for example, the question posed is 'Who was the composer of the opera Don Giovanni?' Several different states of mind and several different response patterns are possible:

1 Definitely known — a fast correct response (Mozart).
2 Definitely not known — a fast response of 'Pass'.
3 Probably not known, or if known very difficult to retrieve — there is a pause for search, followed by a slow response of 'Pass'.
4 Possibly not known but related information is available — this may produce a plausible guess which may turn out to be correct or not.

5 Thought to be known but actually not known — a completely wrong answer is given.
6 Thought not to be known but actually is known — the contestant passes but recalls the answer later.

What processes might underlie these responses? The correct answer in case 1 may be retrieved by consulting a list of composers of opera stored as part of your general knowledge, or by retrieving the memory of a particular visit you made to the opera and remembering the name seen on the programme. The 'definitely not known' response may arise if a rapid scan of memory shows that no opera composers are listed, and there is no record of any visits to the opera. There are some topics we know we know nothing about so that we hardly need to search at all. In cases 1 and 2 metamemory is accurate. The contestant knows what he or she knows or does not know. Uncertain knowledge states like 3 and 4, or outright failures of metamemory like 5 and 6 are less frequent, but can arise when information is in the store but is labelled wrongly or ambiguously so that it is difficult to find. Or the information may be labelled correctly but be so seldom retrieved that it has slipped to the bottom of the file.

It is easier to know what we know when the required fact is directly *pre-stored* in memory. But when a fact is not directly pre-stored, it may still be *computable*. This means it is possible to figure it out indirectly from other facts that are stored. For example, suppose the information 'Mozart is the composer of Don Giovanni' is not pre-stored as such; the correct answer to the question may nevertheless be computed from two other related facts: 'The name of the composer of Don Giovanni begins with an M' and 'A composer whose name begins with M is Mozart'. In this case, the answer has to be inferred rather than being output directly. As a result, computable information generally takes longer to retrieve than pre-stored information and may give rise to greater uncertainty.

An experimental exploration of metamemory by Lachman, Lachman and Thronesberry (1979) is described in Techniques Box B. This is an example of a naturalistic experiment. It was carried out in laboratory conditions but examines knowledge acquired outside the laboratory in everyday life. You can work through the examples as you read it.

This kind of experiment shows that metamemory is generally accurate. Most people are able to direct memory search effectively and not waste time and effort on unproductive searches. These results provide objective evidence that people really do 'know their own memories', and we can therefore feel more confident that questionnaires and diaries are giving us an accurate picture of how memory functions in everyday life.

23

TECHNIQUES BOX B

Lachman, Lachman and Thronesberry's Metamemory Experiment
(1979)

Rationale
The experiment demonstrates that when people don't know a particular fact they can estimate accurately how close they are to knowing it.

Method
The experiment was divided into three phases.

Phase 1: Question answering   Subjects had to answer 190 general knowledge questions covering current events, history, sport, literature, etc. Instructions were: Do not guess; give the answer or respond 'don't know' as fast as possible. Time to respond was measured.
   Try answering these examples of the questions yourself:
(a) What was the former name of Muhammad Ali?
(b) What is the capital of Cambodia?

Phase 2: 'Feeling of knowing' (FOK) judgements   Subjects were represented with all the questions to which they had responded 'don't know' and asked to make a 'feeling of knowing' judgement by ticking one of the following alternatives (1–4) for each question.
   If you don't know the answer to questions (a) or (b) or both, tick the alternative that corresponds to *your* 'feeling of knowing':
Definitely do not know   (1)
Maybe do not know   (2)
Could recognize the answer if told   (3)
Could recall the answer if given hints and more time   (4)

Phase 3: Multiple choice and confidence ratings   After a short delay subjects were presented with a multiple choice of four alternatives for each of the questions to which they had responded 'don't know' and had to select one of these and give a confidence rating for the correctness of the choice. Values 1–4 reflect increasing confidence.
   Tick which you think is the capital of Cambodia:
Angkor Wat   Phnom Penh   Vientiane   Lo Minh
Indicate whether this is:
A wild guess   (1)   Probably right   (3)
An educated guess   (2)   Definitely right   (4)

Results
1 The probability of picking the correct answer in Phase 3 increased proportionately with the strength of the 'feeling of knowing' estimate in Phase 2 (see Figure 1.2) — people who ticked (3) or (4) in Phase 2 were more likely to choose the right answer (Phnom Penh) and give a high confidence rating in Phase 3.

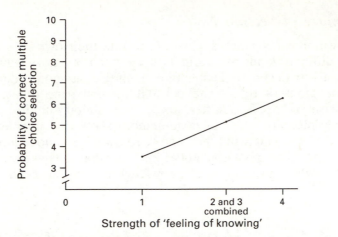

Figure 1.2   Metamemory accuracy: probability of correct recognition as a function of subjective feeling of knowing (adapted from Lachman, Lachman and Thronesberry, 1979, p. 547)

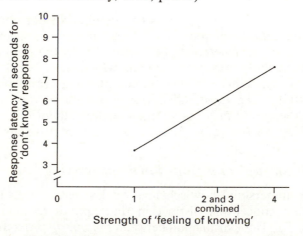

Figure 1.3   Metamemory efficiency: time taken to respond 'Don't know' as a function of subjective feeling of knowing (adapted from Lachman, Lachman and Thronesberry, 1979, p. 547)

2 Response times in Phase 1 were also systematically related to the 'feeling of knowing' in Phase 2 (see Figure 1.3). Subjects searched longer for the items they (mistakenly) thought they might know (FOK values 2, 3 and 4) and terminated the search sooner for items they felt they definitely did not know (FOK value (1)).

3 Confidence ratings in Phase 3 accurately reflected the correctness of the choice. Subjects knew whether they had picked the right answer or only guessed.

Summary of Section 2

- Questionnaires which ask people to rate their own memory ability for different kinds of information show that memory is not good or bad across the board. People rate themselves as good at remembering some kinds of things and poor at remembering others. Memory consists of specific abilities, not a single unitary ability.
- Experimental studies of metamemory show that people are quite good at knowing what they know. Knowledge is not simply present of absent. There is a gradient of knowing that reflects how easily and accurately a given piece of knowledge can be retrieved.

3 Schema theory and everyday memory

It is obvious enough that we do not remember all our experiences in everyday life, and the memories we do retain are not always accurate. They may be vague, incomplete or distorted. Any theoretical approach to everyday memory must try to explain why memory works in this hit-and-miss fashion. What governs the complex pattern of remembering and forgetting? The most influential approach to this fundamental problem has come from *schema theory*. Schema theory emphasizes the fact that what we remember is influenced by what we already know.

3.1 'Bottom-up' and 'top-down' processing

In order to understand how schemas work it is useful to look first at an important conceptual distinction that applies to many cognitive operations. This is the distinction between *bottom-up processing* and *top-down processing*. Very many mental activities like remembering, perceiving and problem solving involve a combination of information from two sources:

1 incoming information from the outside world (i.e. the input received by the sense organs),

and

2 the information already stored in memory (i.e. the prior knowledge derived from past experience).

The analysis of the sensory information coming in from the outside is known as *bottom-up processing* or *data-driven processing* because it relies on the data received via the senses. The sensory information is often incomplete or ambiguous, but the information already stored in the memory in the form of prior knowledge influences our expectations and helps us to interpret the current input. This influence of prior knowledge is known as *top-down* or *conceptually-driven processing*.

In practice the two sorts of processing operate in combination. For example, bottom-up processes may yield sensory information about a moving black shape of medium size and smooth texture. Top-down processes based on already stored knowledge enable this to be identified as a labrador dog. The top-down processes interact with the information provided by the bottom-up processes. This is sometimes known as *interactive processing*.

3.2   What is a schema?

The use of past experience to deal with new experience is a fundamental feature of the way the human mind works. According to *schema theory*, the knowledge we have stored in memory is organized as a set of *schemas** or mental representations, each of which incorporates all the knowledge of a given type of object or event that we have acquired from past experience. Schemas operate in a top-down direction to help us interpret the bottom-up flow of information from the world. New experiences are not just passively copied or recorded into memory. A memory representation is actively constructed by processes that are strongly influenced by schemas.

Bartlett first introduced the notion of schemas as early as 1932 in order to explain how it is that when people remember stories they typically omit some details and introduce rationalizations, reconstructing the story so as to make more sense in terms of their own knowledge and experience. According to Bartlett, the story is 'assimilated' to pre-stored schemas based on previous experience. Although for many years Bartlett's theories were rejected as being too vague, in recent years schemas have been reinstated and have a central role in theories of memory today. Modern versions of schema theory incorporate many of Bartlett's ideas, particularly the idea that what is encoded, stored and retrieved from memory is determined by pre-existing schemas representing previously acquired knowledge. These schemas guide the selection of what aspects of a new input will be stored and may modify the memory representation of a new experience so as to bring it into line with prior expectations and make it consistent with past experience. New experiences in turn can be stored as new schemas or modifications of old schemas, adding to our store of general knowledge.

* The plural of 'schema' is, strictly speaking, 'schemata', but the Open Guides to Psychology use the anglicized version of the original Greek word.

Schemas, then, are packets of information stored in memory representing general knowledge about objects, situations, events, or actions. Rumelhart and Norman (1983) list five characteristics of schemas:

1 Schemas represent knowledge of all kinds from simple knowledge about the shape of the letter 'A', to more complex knowledge such as knowledge about picnics or political ideologies, and knowledge about motor actions like riding a bicycle or throwing a ball.

2 Schemas can be linked together into related systems. An overall schema may consist of a set of sub-schemas. The picnic schema may be part of a larger system of schemas including 'meals', 'outings', and 'parties'. Packets of knowledge about one topic are linked to packets of knowledge about related topics.

3 A schema has *slots* which may be filled with fixed, compulsory values or with variable, optional values. For example, a general schema for a picnic consists of slots for place, food, people, activities, etc. Values are the specific concepts that fill the slots. The place slot takes the fixed value 'outdoors' (by definition), and optional values (such as woods, river, beach) can be added. The values for food, people, etc. are also optional and can be filled according to the particular occasion (see Figure 1.4). Slots may also have *default values*. That is, the schema tells us what probable values the slots can take if specific information is lacking. In the episode shown, the food has not been specified, so the schema supplies 'sandwiches' as a default value for the food slot. Note that, as shown in Figure 1.4, the general picnic schema contains the fixed and default values. The optional values originate from the specific episode.

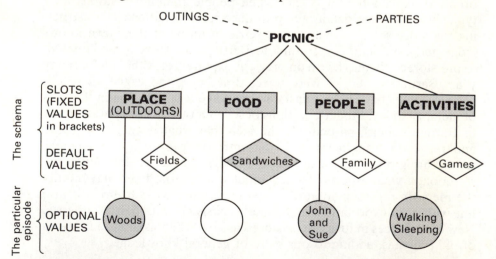

Figure 1.4   A picnic schema: the figure shows how the values supplied by a particular episode mesh with the values supplied by the schema

4 Schemas incorporate all the different kinds of knowledge we have accumulated, including both generalizations derived from our personal experience and facts we have been taught.
5 Various schemas at different levels may be actively engaged in recognizing and interpreting new inputs. Bottom-up and top-down processes may go through repeated cycles, and the final interpretation of new inputs will depend on which schema constitutes the best fit for the incoming information. For example, if we see some people sitting on the grass we might first activate the picnic schema, but if further bottom-up information reveals banners instead of food, we might shift to the 'demo' schema instead. In this case the demo schema turns out to be the best fit and becomes the dominant or most active schema.

This list of characteristics defines a schema in broad general terms. More closely specified versions of schemas are called *scripts* (which consist of general knowledge about particular kinds of events) and *frames* (which consist of general knowledge about the properties of particular objects and locations). For the moment we can use the broader term 'schema' to cover the whole range of stored general knowledge.

3.3 How do schemas affect memories?

When applied to real-life experiences, schemas may influence memory in any of five different ways:
1 *Selection and storage*: The schema guides the selection of what is encoded and stored in memory. Information that is not relevant to the schema that is currently the most active may be ignored. So you may not remember what clothes you wore when taking an exam, because clothes are not relevant to the activated exam schema. As well as guiding selection, the schema also provides a framework within which new information relevant to that schema can be stored.
2 *Abstraction*: Information in memory tends to undergo transformation from the specific to the general. So if you try to recall the occasion of a particular visit to a restaurant you tend to recall the general features common to many such visits rather than the specific details of a particular visit. Only the general schema is retained in memory, while the particular episode is forgotten. Similarly, in remembering conversations or stories you tend to retain the gist or general meaning, but not the exact wording.
3 *Integration and interpretation*: According to schema theory a single integrated memory representation is formed which includes information derived from the current experience, prior knowledge relating to it, the default values supplied by the appropriate schemas, and

any interpretations that are made. The memory of a scene in a restaurant might consist of the original observations — a diner refuses a dish brought to him, and the waiter takes it away; plus the interpretation — that the customer was complaining that something was wrong with the food. This interpretation is based on prior knowledge about possible ways of behaving in restaurants, and the likely reasons for, and outcome of, such behaviour. The observations, the interpretations and the prior knowledge are integrated in the memory representation and may be impossible to distinguish later. In this way we use schema-based knowledge to infer much that is not actually seen or explicitly stated. We fill in missing information, we try to make sense of what is not readily comprehensible, we infer the reasons, causes and results of the events we witness.

4 *Normalization*:   Memories of events also tend to be distorted so as to fit in with prior expectations and to be consistent with the schema: they are therefore transformed toward the most probable, or most typical event of that kind. People may misreport an event they witnessed because they remember what they expected to see rather than what they actually saw. For example, a witness may report that a bank-robber wore a mask when actually he wore dark glasses. The witness's memory was distorted by a schema based on films of bank-robberies.

5 *Retrieval*:   Schemas may also aid retrieval. People may search through the appropriate schema in order to try to retrieve a particular memory. If the required information is not represented directly, it may be possible to retrieve it indirectly, through schema-based inferences. So, if you cannot remember what John and Sue ate at the picnic, the schema supplies the value 'sandwiches' which has a good chance of being correct.

Note especially that whereas the processes of selection, abstraction and normalization explain how information may be lost or reduced in memory, the processes of integration and interpretation and inference-based retrieval serve to enrich and elaborate the memory trace.

3.4   *Some problems with schema theory*

Schema theorists are not very clear as to whether the processes of selection, abstraction, integration and normalization take place at the time the memory is encoded, while it is in store, or at the time the memory is retrieved. Suppose your memory of a family party contains no record that a cousin was present. Did you fail to note his presence at the time, or did you excise him from the representation at some later date? Additions, deletions, interpretations and distortions may be made when the memory representation is originally constructed, or the representation may be tinkered with at some subsequent time when it is reconstructed for recall. Schema-driven encoding and schema-driven reconstruction would produce very similar results and are therefore hard to distinguish.

Anderson and Pichert (1978) devised a very ingenious experiment to test whether schemas operate at encoding or at retrieval.

TECHNIQUES BOX C

Anderson and Pichert's 'Changing Schemas' Experiment (1978)

Rationale
The idea was to supply subjects with one schema at the encoding stage and then give them a new, different schema at the retrieval stage. If schemas only operate at encoding, then the new schema should not influence recall.

Method
Subjects were given a story about two boys who played truant from school and spent the day at the home of one of them because the house was always empty on Thursdays. The story described the house as being isolated and set in attractive grounds. Various objects in the house such as a ten-speed bike, a colour TV, and a rare coin collection were mentioned, as well as features of the house such as a leaking roof and a damp basement. The story contained 72 ideas which were rated by a separate set of non-experimental subjects for their importance to either a potential house-purchaser (e.g. leaking roof, attractive grounds) or a burglar (e.g. coin collection, nobody home on Thursdays). Half the experimental subjects were told to read the story from the point of view of a house-purchaser (i.e. with the buyer schema) and half from the point of view of a burglar (i.e. with the burglar schema).

After a 12-minute delay, filled by a distracting task, recall was tested. There was then a further 5-minute delay. Half the subjects were then given a new schema: those with the buyer schema were switched to the burglar schema and vice versa. The other half of the subjects retained their original schema. Recall was then tested once again.

Results
The changed schema group recalled 7 per cent additional ideas on the second recall test. Recall of ideas important to the new schema increased by 10 per cent. Recall of ideas important to the previous schema declined.

The group who did not have a changed schema actually recalled fewer ideas at the second recall test than at the first recall test.

Conclusions
Schemas must have some effect at retrieval as well as at encoding since the new schema, which was only given at the retrieval stage, produced additional recall. The experiment also shows that people do encode some information which is irrelevant to their prevailing schema, since those who had the buyer schema at encoding were able to recall burglar information when the schema was changed (and vice versa).

Another objection to schema theory is that the whole idea of a schema is too vague to be useful. A structure that is general enough to represent such a variety of different kinds of knowledge must be so unspecified that it is hard to say anything about what it is like.

Critics of schema theory also object that it over-emphasizes the inaccuracy of memory and overlooks the fact that complex events may sometimes be remembered in very precise and exact detail. Schema-driven processes of the kind described above are good at accounting for memory imperfections, but have difficulty in accounting for a memory representation that is accurate in every detail, or one that retains unusual or unexpected elements. People often do remember what is odd or peculiar. Out of all your visits to the dentist, the one that sticks in your memory best is the one when you fell down the stairs. Out of all your visits to restaurants, it is the one when you quarrelled with your partner and walked out that you remember. Yet these occasions are exceptional and fail to conform to the schemas.

Another problem is that it is difficult to see how schemas are acquired in the first place. How do children manage to interpret and remember a completely novel experience when they have no prior knowledge about it, and no schema to guide the interpretations and shape the memory representations? How are schemas built up out of these unstructured experiences? Katherine Nelson (1986) has carried out extensive research on how children acquire schemas.

Finally, there are problems concerning the selection of the most appropriate schema. What ensures that a new input is recognized and interpreted by the right schemas? The suggestion is that those schemas that are the best match are somehow selected, but this explanation glosses over some serious difficulties.

Summary of Section 3

- Schemas are packets of stored knowledge (memory representations) derived from past experience.
- New memory representations of events, scenes and objects are the product of both stored schemas and current input.
- The bottom-up information derived from the senses about an on-going event is interpreted by the top-down influence of relevant schemas so as to construct a memory representation that fits in with prior expectations and past experience.
- As a result, memories of particular events tend to be transformed toward a typical or 'normalized' form.

4   Memory for scenes and events

Schema theory can be best evaluated by looking at some particular studies of everyday memory. How well do people remember the events and scenes they experience in everyday life? To what extent do pre-stored schemas influence what they recall?

4.1   Remembering scenes

The influence of schemas on memory for scenes has been neatly demonstrated in an experiment by Brewer and Treyens (1981) as described in Techniques Box D.

TECHNIQUES BOX D

Brewer and Treyens' Experiment Testing Memory for Objects in a Room (1981)

Rationale
The idea behind the experiment was that people's memory for a scene is influenced by the schema appropriate for that particular scene. In this experiment the scene was a room full of objects. Brewer and Treyens predicted that people would remember those aspects of the scene that they would expect to find in that context and forget items that they would not expect to be there.

Method
Thirty subjects attended one at a time to serve in the experiment. When they arrived they were asked to wait briefly in an office.
    The room was designed to look like a typical graduate student's

---

office with many of the items you would expect to find there (desk, typewriter, coffee-pot, calendar, etc.). Other items did not conform to the office schema (a skull, a piece of bark, a pair of pliers). Schema-expectancy ratings for each object were obtained previously by asking 15 different subjects to rate on a six-point scale 'how likely the object would be to appear in room of this kind'. After 35 seconds waiting in the office the experimental subjects were called into another room and given the unexpected task of writing down everything they could remember having seen in the office.

Results

Most subjects successfully recalled the items with high schema-expectancy ratings (like the desk), and few subjects recalled the items with low schema-ratings (like the pliers). Some subjects falsely recalled things likely to be in a typical office, but not actually present in this one, such as pens, books and a telephone. Memory for the scene was therefore strongly influenced by the pre-existing office schema and, when they came to recall, subjects were supplying default values from this schema. Nevertheless, one or two of the objects which had very low schema-expectancy ratings, like the skull, were recalled by a significant number of subjects, showing that recall is not entirely schema-based.

SAQ 2

Suppose you had been in somebody's kitchen and were later asked to recall objects in it. Which of the following would you be most likely to recall? Which would you be most likely to forget?

    Cooker, sink, hat, teapot, stethoscope.

What other objects might you falsely recall having seen?

4.2   Modifications of schema theory

The *schema-plus-tag model* has been developed (Graesser and Nakamura, 1982) to account for the fact that schema-irrelevant information is sometimes retained as well or better than schema-relevant information. The unusual or atypical item or event may be more memorable than what is predictable or routine. You do remember the unexpected objects in a scene; you remember novel deviations from familiar experiences so, as noted before, of all your visits to the dentist, the one that is particularly memorable is the occasion when you fell down the dentist's stairs. And you also remember one-off unique experiences, like getting married or passing your driving test.

    According to the schema-plus-tag model, the memory representation for a specific event includes both the general schema and distinctive tags or markers labelling any irrelevant or unexpected aspects of the event. So the picnic schema in Figure 1.4 might carry the tag 'Sue fell in the river' to mark a specific occasion. This amended version of schema theory fits both the experimental findings and our common-sense intuitions. Schank (1981) has also modified his original ideas about scripts so as to clarify the relationship between general know-ledge schemas and memory for specific episodes. He has proposed a hierarchical arrangement of memory representations called *MOPS*, or *Memory Organization Packets*. The lowest level of the hierarchy is the most specific and representations at this level store specific details about particular events. At higher levels the representations become progress-ively more general and schema-like. According to the model, low-level specific memories are not usually retained for very long. These specific event memories are absorbed into higher level generalized event memories (schemas) which store the features common to repeated experience. However, in Schank's model, details of particular events are retained if the event is peculiar or untypical in any way. So Schank's MOPs make provision for storing memories of specific episodes as well as general schemas. A model like this is clearly better fitted to account for everyday memory.

4.3   Eye-witness testimony

Eye-witness testimony has been investigated by means of naturalistic experiments — that is, experiments that try to mimic real-world situ-ations while at the same time controlling the relevant variables. These experiments are concerned to assess the accuracy of eye-witness testi-mony. How accurately can people describe an event they witnessed some time previously? What factors are liable to make their reports more accurate or less accurate? These questions are not just academic. They are of paramount importance to the police and to the courts.

Much of the work on eye-witness testimony has been done by Eliza-beth Loftus and her colleagues. Typical examples of her experiments are shown in Techniques Box E.

TECHNIQUES BOX E

Two Experiments in Eye-Witness Testimony

1   Loftus (1975)

Rationale
The experiment tests the theory that new information is integrated with pre-stored memory representations. Specifically, it tests whether people's memory of an event they have witnessed can be falsified if they are later given misleading information about the event.

Method

The experiment consisted of three phases:

Phase 1   150 people (the subjects in the experiment) viewed a film showing a car accident.

Phase 2   Immediately afterwards all the subjects answered ten questions about the event. Subjects had been divided into two groups, A and B. Subjects in Group A received questions, all of which incorporated accurate information about the event, and were *consistent* with what they had seen (e.g. 'How fast was the white sports car going when it passed the "Stop" sign?'). Subjects in Group B received the same questions except for one which contained inaccurate *misleading* information (i.e. 'How fast was the white sports car going when it passed the barn when travelling along the country road?'). (N.B. the film *had* shown the car passing a 'Stop' sign, but there was *no* barn. Mentioning a barn is misleading because it implies that there was a barn.)

Phase 3   One week later all the subjects were asked ten new questions about the accident. The final question was 'Did you see a barn?'

Results

In Group A only 2.7 per cent of the subjects responded 'Yes' to the Phase 3 question about the barn.

In Group B 17.3 per cent responded 'Yes'.

The misleading information had a significant influence on memory of the event. For a considerable number of Group B subjects, the fictitious barn had apparently been integrated with the memory representation of the filmed event.

2   *Loftus, Miller and Burns (1978)*

The rationale is the same as in the previous experiment.

Method

Phase 1   195 subjects viewed a sequence of 30 colour slides depicting events leading up to a car accident.

Group A saw the sequence with the upper picture in Figure 1.5 showing a red Datsun stopped at a 'Stop' sign.

Group B saw the same sequence except that it contained the lower picture showing the Datsun stopped at a 'Yield' sign.

Phase 2   Immediately afterwards all subjects answered 20 questions. For half the subjects in each group Question 17 was:

'Did another car pass the red Datsun while it was stopped at the "Stop" sign?'

For the other half Question 17 was:

'Did another car pass the red Datsun while it was stopped at the "Yield" sign?'

So for half the subjects the question was *consistent* with the slide they had seen and for half the subjects it was *misleading* (inconsistent).

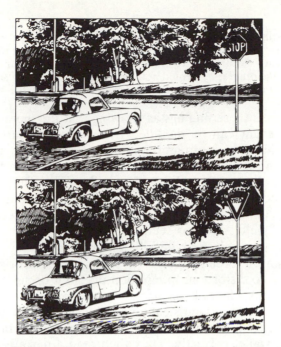

Figure 1.5   The red Datsun at the 'Stop' sign (top) and at the 'Yield' sign (bottom) (Drawings of the photos used by Loftus, Miller and Burns)

Phase 3   20 minutes later there was a forced-choice recognition test. 15 pairs of slides were presented. One of each pair was 'old' (i.e. it had been shown in the original sequence) and one was 'new' (i.e. it had not been seen before). Subjects had to select the 'old' slides. The critical pair of slides showed the 'Stop' sign and 'Yield' sign.

Results
75 per cent of the subjects who had received consistent information in Phase 2 chose the correct slide (i.e. the one with the sign they had seen in the original sequence).

Only 41 per cent of the subjects who had received misleading information were correct (that is, 59 per cent chose the sign mentioned in the question although it was *not* the one seen in the original sequence).

A further experiment showed that if Phases 2 and 3 were both delayed for one week, and administered so that the misleading information came just before the test, then accuracy in the misleading condition fell to 20 per cent. Note that in Loftus (1975) false information was *added* to the memory representation. In Loftus *et al.* (1978) the correct information was *deleted* and *replaced* by the false information.

SAQ 3
In another Loftus experiment, subjects watched a film of a car accident. Subjects in Group A were then asked, 'What speed was the car travelling when it smashed into the other car?' Group B were asked, 'What speed was the car travelling when it bumped into the other car?' Would both groups be likely to give similar estimates of the speed? If not, which group might give a higher estimate? Why?

Loftus interprets these findings as showing that the memory representation of an event can be modified by subsequent information. She claims that this new information is incorporated into the memory, updating it, and erasing any of the original information that is inconsistent with it. According to Loftus, once the new misleading information is integrated into the original memory the subject cannot distinguish its source. He or she actually believes that the non-existent barn or the non-existent 'Yield' sign was seen.

Witnesses cannot always be easily misled. Further experiments (e.g. Loftus, 1979) have revealed conditions which make the original memory more resistant to distortion. Integration does not occur if the misleading information is 'blatantly incorrect'. In one experiment, subjects saw colour slides showing a man stealing a red wallet from a woman's bag. When asked questions about this event, 98 per cent remembered the colour of the wallet correctly. They then read a narrative description of the event containing the misleading information that the wallet was brown. The final test showed that all but two of the subjects resisted this 'blatantly incorrect' information and continued to remember the wallet as red. Thus, memory for obviously important information which is accurately perceived at the time is not easily distorted. The colour of the wallet was correctly remembered because the wallet was the focus of the whole event, not just a peripheral detail, and its colour was correctly noted at the initial viewing. The experiment also demonstrated that once subjects recognized one piece of misleading information as false they were more distrustful and less likely to be misled by any other false information.

We can now summarize these findings. People are more likely to be misled by false information if:
1 It concerns insignificant details that are peripheral to the main event.
2 The false information is given after a delay, when the memory of the actual event has had time to fade.
3 They are not aware that they may be deliberately misinformed and so have no reason to distrust the information they receive.
So the integration of related memories is more likely to take place in some circumstances than in others. New information may sometimes be disregarded and the original memory representation may remain intact. Research on eye-witness testimony has concentrated on the fallibility of memory and so gives rather a one-sided picture.

How far do the findings about eye-witness testimony support the predictions from schema theory? They have often been cited as providing a demonstration of the sort of integration that is predicted by schema theory (Alba and Hasher, 1983). But it should be emphasized that Loftus's misled witnesses are not only integrating prior knowledge from internal schemas about car accidents or purse-snatching with knowledge derived from recently observed event. They are also combining information from two different external sources — an observed event and subsequent verbal information about it — so that the memory may sometimes be a composite based on different sources of information. This kind of integration is not necessarily schema-based.

Nevertheless, eye-witness testimony can be influenced by schemas. Just as Brewer and Treyens showed that schemas can induce people to 'remember' non-existent objects in a room, List (1986) showed that schemas can exert similar effects on memory for events. Her subjects watched videos of shop-lifting incidents. Each incident included some actions rated as having high probability in a shop-lifting scenario and some actions having low probability. The influence of the schema was evident when recall was tested one week later. The subjects recalled more high probability actions and also falsely recalled some actions which had not occurred at all but which were highly likely in a shop-lifting incident. Notice, however, that eye-witness memory is not all schema-based. In the Loftus experiment, recall of the colour of the red wallet is an instance of memory for highly specific information which could not be predicted from a general schema.

Although most of the work on eye-witness testimony has been concerned to demonstrate its unreliability, some attempts have also been made to improve witnesses' recall. Geiselman *et al.* (1985) have devised a technique for interviewing which incorporates four principles based on what cognitive psychologists know about retrieval, and this technique is now known as the *Cognitive Interview*. The principles are:

1 Mentally reinstating the environmental and personal context at the time the event was witnessed. The witnesses are encouraged to 'think back' and recall immediately preceding events, their own actions and their mood.
2 Encouraging them to report every detail however trivial.
3 Asking them to describe the event sequence in different orders, both forward and backward.
4 Asking them to describe the event from different viewpoints (e.g. to say what they would have seen if they had been standing the other side of the road).

These principles are designed to maximize the number of possible retrieval routes. The idea is that reactivating the context will cue the memory of the original event. Experimental tests comparing Geiselman's

39

method with standard interview techniques have shown that up to 30 per cent more information is recalled without loss of accuracy and some police forces in both the USA and the UK are being trained to use the cognitive interview. In the experiments on eye-witness testimony many of the errors occur because subjects are forced to respond 'Yes' or 'No' to direct questions. In real-life situations, when open-ended questions are used, and witnesses can respond 'Don't know' or 'Not sure', testimony is much more accurate.

The most important theoretical point to arise out of the work on eye-witness testimony concerns the fate of the original memory when recall has been influenced by misleading information. This question has relevance to general theories about memory, not just to the eye-witness situation. Do memories get discarded when they are proved false, or are they still retained along with the new revised version? In the context of the work on eye-witness memory several hypotheses have been considered:

1 *The vacant-slot hypothesis* claims that the original information was never stored at all, so the false misleading information is simply inserted into a vacant slot in the memory representation. This hypothesis has been rejected because 90 per cent of subjects who are tested immediately after witnessing an event, and are not exposed to any misleading information, do report the original information correctly.

2 *The co-existence hypothesis* states that both the original true version and the false misleading version are retained in memory and co-exist. According to this hypothesis subjects usually respond with the false version because this was presented more recently and is therefore more accessible.

3 *The substitution hypothesis* states that the false misleading information displaces or transforms the original true information which is then irrecoverably lost. This is the hypothesis favoured by Loftus.

Note that according to (1) and (3) the original memory cannot be recovered but according to (2) the original memory is recoverable. Two techniques have been used to try to resolve this issue, the warnings technique and the second guess technique. In studies examining the effects of warnings, subjects are given false misleading information and then warned that it is false and should be disregarded. The question then is can they reinstate the original memory? This is an important issue which arises in the context of jury decisions. Can jurors discount the evidence of a witness who is later discredited? The answer seems to be that they cannot. Experiments have shown that subjects who were warned to disregard the false information did no better than subjects who were not warned. They could not discard the false information and recover the original memory.

Another way to test whether the original memory is intact is to offer subjects the chance of a second guess. According to the co-existence hypothesis, people whose first response was the false misleading information should be able to make the correct response if given a second guess. Loftus (1979) reported an experiment in which subjects saw, in phase 1, a man reading a green book. The misleading information in phase 2 described the book as yellow. When the subjects were tested in phase 3, they were offered the alternatives green, blue and yellow to choose from. Misled subjects whose first choice was yellow were given a second choice, but their performance on this second guess was only at chance level, showing that they could not recover the original memory of the green book.

On the whole, evidence for the recoverability of the original memory is very slight, so there is little support for the co-existence hypothesis and the substitution hypothesis is more likely to be correct.

4.4   Confusing implications and assertions

Besides confusing what we have seen with what we have been told, we also make similar confusions about the verbal information we receive.

A common form of confusion occurs when people make what are called *constructive errors* in the recall of verbal information. When information is comprehended and stored in memory, the memory representation includes what was directly asserted as well as additional information that is generated from pre-stored schemas. People later fail to remember what was actually asserted (the external source) and instead report what was only implied and then constructed internally. So sentences like:

1 *The housewife spoke to the manager about the increased meat prices.*
2 *The paratrooper leaped out of the door.*
may be remembered as:
3 *The housewife complained to the manager about the increased meat prices.*
4 *The paratrooper jumped out of the plane.*
(Harris and Monaco, 1976)

The new bits that have appeared in (3) and (4) are called *pragmatic implications*. The statement that the paratrooper leaped out of the door implies that he was jumping out of a plane. Schemas about what paratroopers normally do supply this information. People elaborate the information they receive by making inferences of this kind and cannot afterwards distinguish between what was explicitly stated and what was implied. If the inferences drawn are not correct (e.g. if the housewife was in fact only chatting and not complaining), an inaccurate memory is stored.

41

Harris (1978) ran an interesting experiment to investigate how the members of a jury may be influenced by pragmatic implications, and believe that something which has only been implied has actually been asserted as definitely true.

TECHNIQUES BOX F

Harris's (1978) Experiment on Courtroom Testimony

Rationale
Harris tried two ways of making people less inclined to believe that something had been asserted as true when it had only been implied. One was to instruct them not to confuse implications with assertions, and the other was to let them confer together like a real jury in the hope that at least one of the group would detect the implications.

Method
72 subjects listened to a simulated courtroom testimony lasting five minutes. Subjects were told to pretend they were members of a jury. They should listen to the evidence and would be asked questions. Half the subjects had no further instructions. Half were told to be careful not to be influenced by implications but only by the facts and were given detailed examples of how beliefs can be affected by implications. In the testimony some of the information was expressed as direct assertions and some was only implied. Subjects heard different versions of the testimony. For example, some of the subjects heard a version with the direct assertion 'I rang the burglar alarm in the hall', and some heard a version with the statement 'I ran up to the burglar alarm in the hall', which implies that the alarm was rung but does not actually say so. After hearing the testimony, subjects were asked to rate 36 test statements as true, false or of indeterminate truth value (i.e. uncertain). Some subjects worked on their own; others worked together in small groups.

For the test statement 'I rang the burglar alarm in the hall' subjects should have responded 'True' if they had heard the version of the testimony in which it was asserted. If they had heard the implied version they should have judged the truth value as indeterminate.

Results
The mean percentage of 'True' responses to Assertions and Implications are shown in the table.

	Groups	
	No instructions	Instructions
Assertions judged as 'True' (correct)	87.6	80.2
Implications judged as 'True' (incorrect)	67.3	60.4

Altogether 64 per cent of the Implications were incorrectly judged 'True'. Moreover the instructions failed to reduce the number of 'True' responses to Implications by a significant extent. When subjects were allowed to make their decisions in small groups, there was also no significant improvement in accuracy.

Harris concluded that it is dangerously easy to mislead juries into believing that what is only implied is true. In his experiment subjects assumed that someone running up to a burglar alarm would ring it. An implication of this kind is incorporated into the memory representation and afterwards the information that was *heard* and the information that was *thought* (i.e. the implication) cannot be distinguished.

The results demonstrate integration of information from the senses with information derived from inferences based on the prior knowledge of what is likely to occur. Just as predicted by schema theory, it is often impossible to identify the original source of information in the memory representation.

Summary of Section 4

- When people remember a particular scene they are influenced by the schema appropriate for that type of scene. They remember things that fit the schema and forget the things that do not.
- Experiments on eye-witness testimony show that the memory of an event that was witnessed can be falsified if misleading information is presented later.
- It is not clear whether the original memory of the event is changed or whether it remains intact but is superseded by a new, inaccurate memory representation. However, the evidence suggests that it is rarely possible to recover the original memory once it has been tampered with.
- In remembering verbal information, facts that were only implied (and are not necessarily true) may be confused with facts that were actually stated.

5 Absentmindedness and confusions

We have already seen that we can learn a lot about memory by studying the kind of mistakes that we make. Some of these mistakes arise out of failures to carry out plans and intentions correctly.

5.1 Slips of action

Everyday memory does not only consist of a record of past events. As well as remembering what has happened in the past we also use memory in everday life to remember *plans*: to keep track of ongoing actions and of the actions we intend to carry out in the future. Failure to keep track of these plans, is usually called absentmindedness and gives rise to slips of action.

Questionnaires may be used to study absentmindedness with questions like 'How often do you go into a room to do something and forget why you went?' or 'How often do you forget whether you have done something like locking up or switching off the lights so that you have to go back and check?'

Another method which also relies on self-assessment is the diary study. Reason (1979) asked 35 volunteers to keep a diary record of *slips of action*, a term he gave to unintended or accidental actions. In two weeks the diaries yielded 400 of these slips which Reason divided into four categories.

1 *Repetition errors*: Forgetting that an action has already been performed and repeating it, e.g. 'I started to pour a second kettle of boiling water into the teapot, forgetting I had just filled it'. (40 per cent of slips were of this kind.)
2 *Goal switches*: Forgetting the goal of a sequence of actions and switching to a different goal, e.g. 'I intended to drive to one place but then I "woke up" and found I was on the road to another different place', or 'I went upstairs to fetch the dirty washing and came down without the washing having tidied the bathroom instead'. (20 per cent of slips.)
3 *Omissions and reversals*: Component actions of a sequence are omitted or wrongly ordered, e.g. filling the kettle but failing to switch it on, or putting the lid on a container before filling it. (18 per cent of slips.)
4 *Confusions and blends*: Confusing objects involved in one action sequence with objects from another action sequence, e.g. taking a tin-opener instead of scissors into the garden to cut flowers; or wrongly combining actions from different action sequences, like the woman who reported throwing her earrings to the dog and trying to clip

dog-biscuits on her ears. (16 per cent of Reason's errors were confusions of this kind.)

(The remaining slips were unclassifiable.)

However, the reported percentages may be misleading. A particular kind of slip may be reported as more frequent because it is more disruptive and therefore more noticeable.

SAQ 4
Which of Reason's categories do the following slips of action belong to? Explain why.

(a) Pouring tea into the sugar bowl instead of a cup.
(b) Sealing an envelope before putting the letter inside.
(c) Cleaning teeth instead of putting on lipstick.

The important finding is that slips of action mainly occur with highly practised, over-learned routine activities. These highly practised actions become *automatic* and are carried out according to pre-set instructions with little or no conscious monitoring. Automatic actions differ from *attentional* actions which are under moment-to-moment control by a central processor which monitors and guides the sequence. A good example of this distinction between *automatic and attentional processes* occurs when you are driving a car. Emerging from a road junction is (or ought to be) an attentional process. The traffic must be scanned, distances and speeds assessed, and the driver is consciously thinking about the situation and about the decisions he or she is making. For the practised driver, changing gear is an automatic process. The actions involved do not need to be consciously monitored, and can usually be carried out successfully while the driver is attending to something quite different, like chatting with a passenger or thinking about a problem.

Automatic action sequences have the advantage that they can be carried out while conscious attention is freed to engage in some other parallel activity. However, automatization may lead to errors. An action sequence (or program) that is in frequent use is 'stronger' than one that is used less often. There appears to be a tendency for a stronger program to take over a weaker program, particularly if they share component stages. Slips of action like those Reason describes often occur at junctions between stages when there is a switchover to the wrong program. William James (1899) describes a 'strong habit intrusion' of this kind in the case of someone going to the bedroom to change their clothes, taking off one garment and then getting undressed and going to bed. The 'going to bed' program took over from the 'changing clothes' program because both shared the common action of removing the jacket. Besides strong habit intrusions, slips result from losing track of the sequence, with the effect that actions may be omitted or repeated or there may be cross-talk between two concurrent action sequences. Some individuals are much more prone to make these kinds of errors than other people, but everybody finds that slips of action increase with tiredness and stress.

Verbal slips, like spoonerisms or saying one word when you meant to say another, are perhaps more common than action slips and can be categorized and explained in the same sort of way.

Norman (1981) has outlined a theoretical explanation based on schema theory for absentminded slips of action. In his model, action sequences are controlled by schemas. Norman's model emphasizes the *hierarchical organization* of schemas which work together in organized groups as in Figure 1.6.

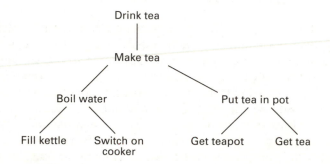

Figure 1.6   A hierarchy of action schemas for making tea

These schemas are knowledge structures representing information about motor actions, just as other schemas represent knowledge about places like offices or events like picnics. Several action schemas may be operative simultaneously, and are linked into related sets. The highest level 'parent' schema corresponds to the intention or goal (like 'drinking tea'). Subordinate 'child' schemas or sub-schemas correspond to the component actions in the sequence (like 'boiling water', or 'putting tea in the pot'). Each schema has its own activation level determined both by external events (the current situation) and internal events (plans and intentions). Each schema also has a set of triggering conditions. A given schema operates when the activation level is sufficiently high, and the current situation matches the triggering conditions. So, in my example, the intention to have a drink of tea activates the whole set of goal-related schemas and seeing the kettle might constitute one of the triggering conditions for initiating the boiling-the-water sub-schema.

Slips of action may occur, according to Norman's model, as a result of faulty specification of the overall intention, faulty activation of the schemas, or faulty triggering. So schemas associated with very strong habits (like going to bed in William James's anecdote) may capture the action sequence because they have higher levels of activation than the schemas linked to the original intention (the 'changing clothes' schema).

Reason's goal switches and confusions are obviously very similar to Norman's ideas about faulty triggering. In Reason's example, the triggering conditions encountered on going into the untidy bathroom set off the 'bathroom tidying' schema in place of 'fetching the washing'. Like Reason's categories of slips, Norman's causes of errors are also not very distinct. Driving to the wrong destination may be partly due to inadequate specification of the intention, partly because the activation level of the schema for taking the unintended route is particularly high, and partly because the triggering conditions are appropriate for more than one schema. It seems likely that slips may originate from a combination of all three causes. We noted earlier that a general problem with schema theory concerns the mechanism for selecting the correct schema. Norman's model for slips of action suggests how this mechanism might work and why it sometimes goes wrong.

Vallacher and Wegner (1987) have emphasized that actions can be specified at different levels. Thus, in the tea-drinking action sequence, the actor may specify it in high-level terms as 'taking a break', or at a much lower level in terms of the arm movements required to lift the cup. Maintaining effective action performance depends on the level at which the action sequence is specified by the actor. Vallacher and Wegner showed that while actions are normally specified at higher levels, actors will move to a lower level of specification if the action is difficult, unfamiliar or very complex. For example, the expert driver may specify an action as 'turning right'; the novice will specify it in terms of braking, changing down and steering.

5.2   Prospective memory

Absentmindedness and slips of action are failures of *prospective memory* which is the term used for remembering to do things in the future. *Retrospective memory* involves remembering events experienced in the past, or knowledge acquired in the past, but prospective memory involves remembering to perform actions and carry out plans at some time in the future. In everyday life, prospective memory is crucially important: being able to remember what to do and when to do it is the key to efficient performance. How does prospective memory differ from retrospective memory? The two kinds of memory are not completely distinct. A plan that is stored in prospective memory usually includes a good deal of retrospective knowledge. My plan to buy more cat food on the way home from work includes retrospective knowledge about which shops stock it and about the likes and dislikes of my cats. However, prospective memory ability does not necessarily correlate with retrospective memory ability. Research has shown that people with good retrospective memory may do poorly at a prospective memory task. Subjects who did well on a test for recall of lists of words (retrospective memory) did poorly at remembering to take pills at specified times (prospective memory) (Baddeley, 1990). This phenomenon, known as the 'absentminded professor effect', shows that the two kinds of memory are functionally distinct.

A distinguishing feature of prospective memory is that it involves a time element. A prospective plan contains some indication as to when the plan should be implemented. This may be a specific time (e.g. a dentist's appointment at 4 p.m. next Tuesday) or it may be within some more indefinite period (e.g. before next week, or when the weather improves). Prospective memory includes both the content of the plan and its timing, and implementation of the plan involves time-monitoring as well as remembering what to do. Another feature of prospective memory is that it involves dynamic relationships between plans. Planned actions are sequenced and embedded within each other. A plan to phone a colleague may be sandwiched between a meeting and lunch and be embedded within a higher order plan to enlist the colleague's help. So prospective memory involves keeping track of ongoing action sequences as well as keeping track of time. It may also be necessary to assess the relative priority of competing plans; to scrap those with low priority and to give precedence to implementing those with higher priority. And it is necessary to keep track of which plans have been successfully completed and which are still incomplete or queuing. The amount of attentional control required to implement and monitor plans depends on how far they involve routine familiar actions and how far they consist of novel actions. Routine actions, as we have already noted, may become largely automatic and can then be implemented with minimal demands on prospective memory. Novel actions usually require more attentional control. The process of keeping track of ongoing action sequences which are under attentional control involves the operation of working memory which is described in Part II. Failures of prospective memory often occur because working memory is overloaded with other tasks so that insufficient attentional control is allocated to the task.

Research on prospective memory is of considerable practical importance. For example, the success of medical treatment depends on people being able to remember to take medication or keep appointments, and the safety of nuclear power stations or flying fast jet planes depends on people being able to remember to carry out actions at the right time and in the right order. However, research is complicated by the fact that the memory component is hard to separate from other factors such as motivation and compliance, stress and fatigue. People may fail to carry out a prospective memory task like keeping a hospital appointment because they are poorly motivated, or a pilot may fail to make flight checks because of fatigue.

Some researchers (e.g. Wilkins, 1976) have designed naturalistic experiments such as asking subjects to telephone the researcher or to post postcards at specified times and dates. This method has the advantage of corresponding closely to the everyday use of prospective memory and it allows the experimenter to study the effects of varying time factors, such as the length of time elapsing between instruction and performance, and the number and spacing of the repetitions of phoning or posting. Wilkins instructed his 34 subjects to post their card back after intervals ranging from 2 to 36 days and found no effect of the length of the retention interval. This finding underlines the difference between prospective memory and retrospective memory, since retrospective memory declines as time elapses. It may be difficult, though, to control the strategies people adopt to support prospective memory. When subjects are questioned about how they remember to do these kinds of prospective memory tasks they report using both internal and external reminders. Internal reminders consist of mentally linking the prospective task to some fixed event or habitual activity, like remembering to make a phone call after having lunch. External reminders include making notes in a diary or on a wall chart, making knots in a handkerchief, or leaving an object involved in the task, such as the to-be-posted postcard, in a prominent place. Individuals vary in the extent to which they rely on reminders and in the type of reminders they employ. Another variable which is difficult to control is the lifestyle of the subjects. The performance of people with a very busy lifestyle will tend to be different from that of those who have fewer competing tasks to schedule. For these reasons, prospective memory is an example of an area where it is proving difficult to establish general principles.

Summary of Section 5

- Absentminded slips of action occur when the schema for the wrong action sequence is activated instead of the schema for the correct action sequence.
- Actions are mentally represented in hierarchically organized schemas.
- Prospective memory is remembering to carry out plans or intentions and is distinct from retrospective memory. Prospective memories involve remembering when to perform an action, as well as what to do, and how to order and combine different actions.

6   *Autobiographical memories*

The study of *autobiographical memory* is concerned with how well people can remember personal experiences and events from their past, and focuses on questions such as: What kind of events are remembered best? Do memories change over time? How do we search for and retrieve these memories? How are autobiographical memories organized and retrieved?

6.1   *What is autobiographical memory?*

How can we define autobiographical memory and distinguish it from other types of memory? Before we can begin to answer this question we need to examine a distinction between two kinds of long-term memory, *episodic and semantic memory*. This distinction was first put forward by Tulving in 1972. Semantic memory consists of meaningful facts about the world in general (like the fact that Paris is the capital of France; that birds can fly; that January is the first month of the year). The general knowledge questions in the experiment in Techniques Box B are tapping semantic memory. Episodic memory consists of a record of specific experiences. Tulving originally used this distinction to differentiate between the type of memory tested when people are asked general knowledge questions (semantic) and the type of memory tested when they have to recall lists of unrelated words or nonsense syllables they have learned in an experiment. He considered recall of these lists tapped episodic memory because the process of learning the words constitutes a specific experience or episode. Tulving himself considered that episodic memory is synonymous with autobiographical memory but most people would not consider that learning a list of words in an experiment is what they understand by autobiographical memory. Autobiographical memory is a special kind of episodic memory which is concerned with specific life events which have self-reference; that is, they have personal significance to oneself. For the sake of clarity, therefore, we can distinguish between autobiographical episodic memory and experimental episodic memory. In this section the kind of episodic memory we are concerned with is autobiographical.

Autobiographical episodic knowledge usually includes details about the particular time and particular place in which objects and events were experienced. This is known as the *spatio-temporal context*. General semantic knowledge is not tied to a specific context in this way. In practice, of course, the two kinds of knowledge, episodic and semantic, are very closely interrelated. Tulving (1984) has suggested that episodic memory is embedded within semantic memory. There is a two-way traffic (top-down and bottom-up) between them. Semantic knowledge about weddings is built up from particular episodic experiences of individual weddings by a process of abstraction and generalization. And when you attend a particular wedding, top-town general knowledge is brought to bear in understanding what is going on.

Everyday memory involves both kinds of memory interacting with each other in this way. Everyday experiences are the source of general knowledge; general knowledge allows us to interpret everyday experiences.

You can see how the distinction between episodic and semantic memory is closely related to schema theory. Schemas consist of packets of general semantic knowledge. Much of the knowledge in a schema is derived from repeated episodes, and schemas are used to interpret new episodes. In Figure 1.4, the upper rows represent general semantic knowledge about picnics: the bottom row represents episodic memory of a specific picnic. The episodic–semantic distinction can be represented within schema theory without the need to hypothesize that there are separate systems of episodic and semantic memory. Some psychologists (e.g. McKoon, Ratcliff and Dell, 1986) have been very sceptical of Tulving's claim that there are two different systems. Nevertheless, the distinction between episodic and semantic types of memory has undoubtedly proved a useful one.

| | Episodic memory | | Semantic memory |
	Autobiographical	*Experimental*	
Type of information represented	Specific events, objects, places and people; context-bound	Experimental material, lists; context-bound	General knowledge and facts about events and objects; context-free
Type of organization in memory	Chronological (by time of occurrence) or spatial (by place of occurrence)	Serial order	In schemas (packets of general knowledge relating to the same topic)
Source of information	Perception, personal experiences, life events	Particular experiences as experimental subject	Abstraction from repeated experiences, generalizations learned from others
Focus	Subjective reality (the self); has personal significance	Task specific, no personal significance	Objective reality (the world); no personal significance

How is episodic information treated in memory? There are three possibilities.

1 It may be forgotten quite rapidly.

2 A particular episode may be absorbed into semantic memory contributing to the creation of a schema. The particular details are lost and only a generalized version common to similar episodes is retained.

3 A particular episode may sometimes be retained in episodic memory and remembered in specific detail.

All three of these possibilities can be observed when eye-witnesses are asked to recall events.

Within this framework we can distinguish different types of autobiographical memory. Some autobiographical memories can be classed as *declarative* (i.e. they simply record a particular fact). You may have a declarative memory of the fact that you own a car, that you have dark hair, or that you have a brother. However, many autobiographical memories are *experiential* or *procedural*. When you recall a holiday by the sea you may consciously re-live the experience instead of simply recalling the fact, and your memory may be accompanied by images and emotions. You recall the actions (or procedures) which you performed. When it is re-experienced the event may be 'seen' either from the point of view of the self (i.e. as it was originally experienced) or it may be 'seen' from the viewpoint of an external observer. It has been suggested that highly emotional memories are more often recalled from the observer viewpoint. You can try testing this claim introspectively on your own memories. Autobiographical memories may also differ in specificity. You may have a specific memory of eating dinner with your family on a particular occasion or you may have a generic memory of family dinners. It has also been argued that some autobiographical memories are exact and vivid copies of the original event while others are reconstructions which may have changed over time.

6.2 Diary studies of autobiographical memory

Marigold Linton (1982) undertook a systematic six-year study of her own memory. Every day she wrote on cards a brief description of at least two events that occurred on that day. Every month she re-read two of these descriptions, selected at random from the accumulating pool, and tried to remember the events described, to estimate the order in which they had occurred and the date of each event. She also rated each event for salience (importance) and for emotionality, both at the time of writing the description and again at the time of recall.

To give an idea of how it worked, here is an example. If I were following Linton's procedure I would record 'Took the car into the garage for service' and 'Went to a drinks party given by some new friends' as my two events for yesterday. Both events rate fairly low in importance and emotionality. If, say, two years later, I were to try to remember these events and date their occurrence I doubt very much if I would remember the routine event of taking the car to the garage. I probably would remember the relatively more unusual event of the party given by the neighbours, and would be able to date this by re-membering when they moved into the village.

This is more or less what Linton found. She distinguished two main types of forgetting. One common form of memory loss was associated with repetitions of the same or similar occurrences. Over time there is a decrease in the distinctiveness of these repeated events. Linton de-scribed how she regularly attended committee meetings in another town. Although the first meeting and the most recent meetings remained distinctive, the rest could not be differentiated from each other in memory.

The distinction between episodic and semantic memory explains why this is so. The first trip is a novel episode and generates a lot of epi-sodic information specific to that particular trip. It also utilizes know-ledge from semantic memory. Pre-existing schemas relating to airports, taxis, hotels, committee meetings, supply basic frameworks for storing episodic information about the current event such as the names and faces of fellow committee members, the agenda, and discussion. With repeated occurrences of the meetings there is an increase in general semantic knowledge about them. The elements and patterns that are common to all meetings of that committee are abstracted and absorbed into an expanded general schema which is re-used for each event repetition. As shown in Figure 1.7, the proportion of specific episodic

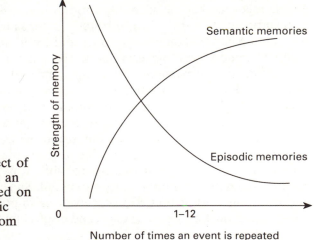

Figure 1.7 The effect of the number of times an experience is repeated on episodic and semantic memory (adapted from Linton, 1982, p. 80)

information distinctive to a particular occurrence shrinks and the proportion of semantic knowledge expands as the number of repetitions increases. Thus, it gets more and more difficult to remember one particular occasion in a succession of repeated events. This type of confusion occurs because there is an integration of different episodes into a general memory schema.

SAQ 5
Decide which of the following can be classified as episodic knowledge and which as semantic knowledge. Explain the reasons for each classification.
(a) It is possible to get from an airport to a hotel by taxi or bus.
(b) At the last meeting the chairman of the committee wore a striped tie.
(c) At committee meetings the members sit around a table.
(d) After the meeting the committee members went to eat at a Chinese restaurant.

Linton's findings that for repeated events like attending meetings she had only a general composite memory and could not recall specific dates and occasions is an example of one type of forgetting, the confusion of similar memories. She also noted a second type of forgetting. When she read the descriptions of some events, she could not remember the event happening at all. Here it is not the case that two or more similar events are confused, but that a single event is simply forgotten. For example, I may fail to remember cutting my finger two years ago. These forgotten events tend to be relatively trivial ones. Linton found that the number of events forgotten in this way increased steadily with each year that elapsed since their occurrence. For recent memories, the two types of forgetting (failure to distinguish between similar events and failure to recall) occurred about equally often, but for events that happened more than two years previously simple recall failure became increasingly frequent. By the sixth year of the study, 30 per cent of the events recorded had been totally forgotten.

A surprising feature of Linton's study is her failure to find any strong relationship between rated importance and emotionality, and subsequent recall. Common sense suggests that we remember important events, or events that roused passions, better than those that were trivial or left us unmoved. However, Linton found that the emotionality and importance ratings she gave to an event initially did not correspond closely with the ones given later. She suggests that events which seem significant when they occur turn out to be unimportant with hindsight. She found it difficult to make accurate and stable judgements about the long-term significance of events, and this is probably why she failed to find a relationship between emotionality and recall. She concludes that events endure in memory if they are perceived as important and are highly emotional at the time of occurrence, and also retain the same significance later in life.

To gain insight into the way events are related and linked together in autobiographical memory, Linton has studied strategies of recall. She tried to recall all the events in a designated month. Introspective monitoring of her own recall attempts showed that many events were organized chronologically and were recalled by reconstructing events in the order in which they occurred. Some events were also organized in categories and were retrieved by working through named categories like social activities, sporting activities, etc. If the events to be recalled were more than two years old, there was a shift away from chronological search toward greater use of categorical search. This shift reflects the fact that time-based episodic memory representations are replaced by category-based semantic memory representations. Recall attempts also revealed that events may be organized in what Linton calls *extendures*. These are continuing situations such as a job or a marriage. Within these extendures specific events and episodes are embedded, and these in turn contain specific elements or details. This hierarchical organization lends itself to top-down search, first accessing the relevant extendure and then homing in on a particular event.

Marigold Linton's study is a prime example of the use of the self-report method. It is also a single case study. Her findings have great intuitive appeal but obviously we should be cautious in generalizing from a single person's introspections.

In another diary study of autobiographical memory, William Wagenaar (1986) recorded 2,400 events over a period of six years. For each event he noted who was involved; what happened; and when and where it occurred. When he came to test his ability to recall the events he presented himself with one of these cues and tried to recall the others. So, for example, the *what* cue might supply the information 'had dinner at a Chinese restaurant', and he would try to recall *when*, *where* and *who*. His results showed that the percentage of questions correctly answered dropped from 70 per cent to 35 per cent over a period of four years. The most powerful cue was *what* followed by *where* and *who*. The *when* cue was almost useless, so these findings suggest that autobiographical memories are organized by category rather than by time of occurrence.

6.3   *Flashbulb memories*

Flashbulb memory is the term that has been given to the kind of vivid and detailed recollection people often have of the occasion when they received a piece of news of public importance, such as being told of the assassination of John F. Kennedy. Brown and Kulik (1982) suggest that there is a neural mechanism triggered by events that are emotional, surprising and highly important or 'consequential'. This mechanism, they claim, causes the whole scene to be 'printed' on the memory.

Neisser (1982) has questioned this account of flashbulb memories. He believes that their durability results from frequent rehearsal and reconsideration after the event, rather than special processes activated at the moment itself. He points out that the importance of an event is sometimes not apparent at the time but is only established later. He also cites cases where flashbulb memories recounted in great detail and good faith turn out to be inaccurate when independently checked. So it is not clear whether we need to attribute the peculiar vividness and durability of these memories to some special mechanism, or whether they are just ordinary memories that survive because they are often reactivated.

Brown and Kulik base their claim that a special mechanism exists for flashbulb memories on the similarity of structure (the *canonical form*) that is exhibited. People remember where they were (Place), what they were doing (Activity), who told them (Informant), and what they felt about it (Affect). According to Neisser, there is no need to postulate a special mechanism to explain these uniformities. They are the product of 'narrative conventions', the traditional schemas that govern the format for story telling. If we accept Neisser's account, schema theory can explain the canonical form of flashbulb memory. The events have simply been slotted into the story-telling schema. Whatever the underlying mechanism, these highly important, significant, and emotionally charged events are selectively well-preserved.

Rubin and Kozin (1984) argue that so-called flashbulb memories are not essentially different in character from other vivid memories. They asked subjects to report their clearest memories and then rate these for importance, surprise, vividness and emotionality. Amongst events recalled, accidents, injuries and encounters with the opposite sex predominated. The vividness of these memories was related to surprise, emotionality and personal importance. Although flashbulb memories are defined as relating to events of *public* importance, these *private* memories of personally important events are very similar.

Activity
Try asking one or two friends (if they are old enough!) what they remember about the occasion when they heard the news of the first moon-landings, or the assassination of John Kennedy. Do their memories conform to the typical structure? Are they especially vivid?

6.4   *Remote memories*

In contrast with vivid and easily recalled flashbulb memories, several recent studies have probed for more elusive and remote autobiographical memories.

One way of doing this is to ask people to recall the names of teachers or classmates from their school days. (In America this information can be verified from high school year books.) The interest of these studies lies not just in the success or failure of the recall attempts, but in the nature of the search processes. The subjects are asked to 'think aloud' as they struggle to recall the information and these running commentaries on the search process (called *verbal protocols*), provide detailed records of the way past experience is stored and organized in memory. Whitten and Leonard (1981) asked 161 university students to recall the name of one teacher from each year at school. They found that backward ordered search was more effective than forward ordered or random search. It was easier to work backwards in time than to start with the first years at school and work forwards, or just to jump about randomly. This result implies episodic memories are not accessed independently. If they were stored and accessed independently a random order of search would be equally successful. Instead memories are interdependent, with memories that are adjacent in time sharing the same context of occurrence and being retrieved together.

In backward search the starting point is the most recent period (the last year at school) and therefore the most easily recalled. Once this is accessed it aids recall of the next-to-last item which shares some of the same context, and so on, in a reverse chaining. As Linton found (in Section 6.2), chronological ordering is apparent in the organization of autobiographical episodic memories. But search is not always chronological. The protocols also revealed that recall often involved imagery including physical attributes of the teachers ('She was a gigantic woman with a scar on her neck') and locations ('I'm thinking about which classrooms I went into'). Some teachers were remembered by the emotional responses they evoked; others were linked to important events in the life of the pupil.

Activity
Try recalling the names of *your* teachers at school. Write a short description (a protocol) of your search processes. Did you work backwards in time? Did you search locations? Why did you remember the particular names that came to mind?

Williams and Hollan (1981) asked four subjects between the ages of 22 and 37 to recall names of classmates. Over testing sessions amounting to 10 hours, the number of names retrieved ranged from 83 (the poorest subject's score) to 214 (the best subject's score). Often the retrieval attempts involved recovery of locations, situations, activities, as subjects tried to generate a context within which to search for names:

'I'm trying to remember the name of this guy who used to — Art —
he was in the 10th grade at art class — he would also bring a whole
lot of people to — At his house was the first time I heard a Jefferson
Airplane album.'

'I remember this girl who used to play the oboe, and it was junior
year, she was our age — or was she older? —'

These contexts allowed the subjects to focus search on a subset of
information. They often speak as if scanning internal images of scenes
and events. As well as the names correctly recalled, many others proved
to be incorrect. Subjects often realized this and corrected themselves.

Summing up the findings, the most striking features of these recall
attempts are as follows:

1 The interconnectedness of memories: one item retrieved leads on to
   another. It is easier to work backwards from the present than forwards from a point in the past.
2 Subjects were able to extend their recall far beyond the limits that
   appeared in the initial session. Information continued to accumulate
   over later sessions, so persistent searching does unearth memories
   that initially seem inaccessible.
3 Retrieval of items from episodic memory depends heavily on re-
   creating the context in which the items were originally embedded.
   General knowledge schemas relating to activities and places (such
   as sporting activities, maths classes, the refectory, etc.) provide the
   framework for these contexts. People use general knowledge about
   what they did in school as a first step in reinstating specific memories.
   This process of reinstatement is the same as that used by Geiselman
   in the Cognitive Interview technique described in Section 4.3.

Norman and Bobrow (1979) have developed a model of retrieval processes that fits well with the findings from these studies. They postulate
three stages in the retrieval of a target item.

1 *Formation of the initial specification.* This consists of the description
   of the target and the context (i.e. a context-dependent description)
   which could be something like 'the dark-haired girl who used to sit
   next to me in geography'. General knowledge schemas are used to
   build the context-dependent descriptions.
2 *Matching a retrieved item against the specification.* An example of this
   process from Williams' and Hollan's data is: 'There was this guy who
   used to sit back of me. He took Spanish classes — His last name
   began with an "O" — the name Orin Elliot sticks —'
3 *Evaluation.* This stage involves judging whether a retrieved item
   really does fit the target specification: 'Linda Turner — that seems
   to fit — the last name for sure I remember.'

These three stages may be repeated in cyclical attempts at retrieval,
with more information being added to the target specification as further

details are remembered. According to Norman and Bobrow, retrievability is a function of constructability (the ability to form an appropriate target description) and discriminability (the ability of that description to discriminate among all possible memories).

Anecdotally, people often claim that they can remember the distant past more vividly than the recent past and it is said to be a characteristic of memory in old age that remote memories are more easily recalled than recent ones. However, these claims have not stood up to experimental tests. The word-cueing method has been used to examine the incidence of memories from different parts of the lifespan. Subjects are presented with a list of cue words and for each word they are asked to think of an autobiographical memory associated with that word. They then describe the memory and date it. Given the cue word 'bicycle', I may recall getting a new bicycle as a tenth birthday present. When a large number of subjects have responded to all the cue words, the number of memories elicited from each period of the lifespan can then be plotted and a *retention function* obtained as shown in Figure 1.8.

Most of the studies using this method have found that the number of memories produced declined with remoteness. Recent memories

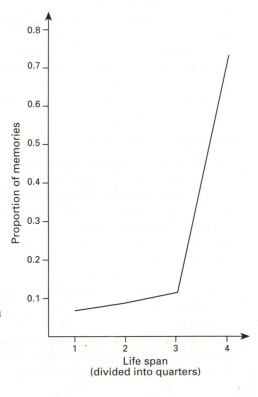

Figure 1.8 Retention function showing the proportion of memories from each quarter of life (adapted from Holding *et al.*, 1986)

are, on the whole, more accessible than remote ones. Other studies have compared the vividness of memories of different ages and confirmed that recent memories are also more vivid than remote ones, and this is true for elderly subjects as well as for young subjects. The popular idea that memories from long ago are well preserved arises because most people have a few favourite memories from their early lives which are especially well preserved because they are often mentally rehearsed or described. When memory for less privileged events is tested a different pattern emerges. Autobiographical memories deteriorate with time.

We can invoke schema theory to explain some of the effects of age on both episodic autobiographical memory and on retention of semantic memory. Memories of early childhood tend to be both sparse and incoherent. Relatively little is recalled of events occurring before the age of seven. This phenomenon is sometimes known as *childhood amnesia*, but we do not need to look for physical or emotional injuries to explain it. A plausible reason is that the young child has not yet developed the general knowledge schemas which are needed to interpret, organize and stabilize early autobiographical memories. Memories of early childhood usually consist of isolated fragments — the tags without the schemas.

At the other end of the lifespan, studies of memory in old age have shown that elderly people who have a lifetime of expertise in a particular semantic memory domain like music or gardening have good retention of information within this domain even when memory for other matters is severely curtailed. The powerful schemas that they have developed support the retention of expert knowledge (Hulicka, 1982).

Summary of Section 6

- Autobiographical memories are *episodic*. They consist of specific events, objects and people personally experienced at particular times and places. *Semantic* memory consists of general knowledge abstracted from these personal experiences and organized into schemas.
- Autobiographical memories which involve repeated occurrences of similar events become difficult to distinguish from each other. The episodic information specific to each event is lost, while the features common to all the repeated incidents are gradually built up into general schemas in semantic memory.
- Trivial events that are of little emotional significance tend to be forgotten.
- Flashbulb memories for events that are important and highly charged emotionally seem to be recalled in vivid detail. This may be due to some special encoding mechanism or to frequent retelling.

- Remote autobiographical memories can be retrieved by using chronological organization and searching backwards in time. Alternatively, general knowledge schemas may be used to reinstate the context of the target and generate a description of the setting, the location, associated activities, physical attributes, etc. The search process is then focused on the relevant context.
- Recent memories can be accessed more easily than remote memories.

7 Conclusions

How does everyday memory work? Of life's rich tapestry (as the saying goes) what do we remember and what do we forget? As we have seen, there is considerable support for an explanation based on schema theory. Memory schemas, loosely defined as frameworks of prior knowledge, appear to exert a far-reaching influence on everyday memory. Schemas control and guide the implementation of plans and actions. They govern the selection of what is important to remember. Previous experiences represented in schemas enable us to supply information that is missing, to make inferences, to guess what we do not know and to reconstruct what we have forgotten. Given that we cannot remember everything, schemas are a powerful device for making the most of what we do remember.

However, the benefits conferred by a schema-based memory system are also accompanied by some disadvantages. Because memories tend to be transformed toward the most probable and most familiar form, mistakes and distortions can occur. Guesses may sometimes be wrong and inferences unwarranted. When new information is integrated with a pre-existing schema it may be impossible to distinguish the old from the new. Implications are sometimes treated as assertions, and probable events may be confused with real events. There is a tendency for specific details to be lost and for similar events to be telescoped in memory into a single general representation. Nevertheless, it is probably true to say that the errors that are introduced into memory by schemas are not serious enough to outweigh the advantages.

It is questionable, though, whether schema theory gives a complete account of everyday memory. Our memories of the events of our daily lives are not always so abstract and generalized as schema theory would predict. Autobiographical episodic memories are sometimes long-lasting, detailed and accurate. We do sometimes remember what is odd or unexpected about an event as well as what is in accordance with our expectations. We may retain vivid memories of first encounters or one-off experiences when there could have been no relevant pre-existing schema to govern our remembering.

In the preceding sections we have outlined various types of memory which are differentiated in terms of the kind of information that is remembered: general knowledge or specific details; autobiographical experiences; witnessed events and future actions. In discussing the results of memory questionnaires we noted that people seem to have different sorts of memory ability. Does this mean, then, that each type of memory is served by a different system? To constitute a separate system there must be a functionally separate mechanism with its own structures and processes. Part II of this book is devoted to two different models of memory systems of this kind: the working memory system (Part IIA) and production systems (Part IIB). It is fairly generally agreed that short-term memory and long-term memory are separate systems (see Eysenck and Keane, 1990, pages 138–41 for a discussion of the evidence). However, although there is considerable evidence for a distinction between episodic and semantic memory, it is not at all clear that episodic and semantic memory constitute separate systems. They may simply represent different levels of hierarchical schemas within the long-term memory system rather than being separate systems.

We noted earlier that prospective memory ability is sometimes dissociated from retrospective memory ability. Prospective memory is not in itself a separate system. However, it is mediated primarily by the working memory system described in Part II, which handles verbal and visual information as well as information about actions. Retrospective memory differs from prospective memory because it is mediated primarily by recall from the long-term memory system. Issues about how many memory systems there are, how far they are functionally independent and how they can be identified are still being debated and no final consensus has yet emerged.

It is easy to criticize everyday memory research as being less 'scientific' than formal laboratory experiments. In trying to study memory in real-world conditions, researchers sacrifice some of the controls they can impose in the laboratory. But, as the studies reviewed here show, research which is carefully designed and cautiously interpreted is yielding findings that are interesting and important both theoretically and practically.

Further reading

Memory in the Real World (1989) by Gillian Cohen covers the same ground as this chapter in a lot more detail and includes other areas of everyday memory as well.

Autobiographical Memory: An Introduction (1990) by Martin Conway provided an in-depth treatment of this topic.

Part IIA
Memory Systems:
The Experimental
Approach

Gillian Cohen (based on an earlier version
by Michael W. Eysenck)

Contents

1   Memory systems

Both Part II, 'Memory systems', and Part III, 'Parallel distributed processing and its application in models of memory', are concerned with models of memory systems.

Part I on 'Everyday memory' was mainly concerned with the *contents* of memory but in the rest of this book the focus shifts more toward memory *mechanisms*. In order to understand how human memory works we need to be able to describe the structures and processes that are involved when memories are input; how they are represented and stored; and how they are retrieved. Models of memory systems are designed to represent these structures and processes.

Part IIA examines systems designed for the short-term storage of information. The specification of short-term memory within a multi-store model of memory outlines some characteristics of its structure and processes, but the more recent model of working memory is a much more detailed short-term system with several component sub-systems. Both models are based on the findings from formal laboratory experiments specifically designed to test hypotheses about them. Part IIB describes production systems and ACT*, a more general model which encompasses both short-term and long-term memory and the transfer of information to and fro between them. Production systems have been developed by modelling the behaviour of subjects engaged in tasks that require memory, rather than on the basis of formal experiments. Both the working memory model and production systems are examples of the functional approach in psychology. That is, they focus on what these systems can do; how they operate in tasks like problem solving, arithmetic and language use. This approach highlights the fact that memory systems are not just storehouses. Memory is central to, and actively engaged in, every cognitive activity.

1.1   Short-term storage of information

Psychologists have generally argued that there is a component of memory that is used for both the short-term storage of information and the active processing of information. Until comparatively recently, the emphasis was very much on the storage function and the component was called the *short-term store*, or *short-term memory*; so that is where we shall begin. In historical terms, the *working memory* model, to be discussed later, evolved out of earlier work on short-term memory.

Is this theoretical interest in short-term memory justified? We can attempt to answer this question by considering the reasons why we have a short-term storage system. Let us try to imagine the consequences of being deprived of it. Many everyday activities would become virtually impossible. For example, it would be extremely difficult to hold a conversation if you were unable to keep in mind what had just been said. In the same way, when thinking about some complicated problem, it is very useful to have available a short-term system that will store information about part of the problem briefly while you concentrate on other parts of the problem.

Activity
Attempt to work out the answers to the questions below purely by means of mental arithmetic (i.e. doing all the workings in your head).

(1)   6 + 9   (2)   26 + 78   (3)   443 + 65 + 9

While you probably answered Question 1 without needing to rely on short-term storage of any part of the problem, most people find that Question 3 requires a certain amount of short-term storage of parts of the answer during problem solution. If you had to do this, can you remember exactly what information you held in short-term storage? Question 2 represents an interesting 'half-way' house. Some people can answer such a question fairly directly, whereas others tackle it in two or three stages, storing parts of the answer as they proceed.

1.2   The multi-store model of memory

The first systematic attempt to incorporate the notion of a short-term store within a general theory of memory was by Atkinson and Shiffrin (1968, 1971). As can be seen in Figure 2.1, they proposed three kinds of memory store: *sensory registers*, *short-term memory*, and *long-term memory*. This *multi-store model*, often known as the *modal model*, is described in more detail elsewhere (e.g. Cohen, 1990), but its main characteristics will be sketched in here. In essence, it is assumed that input information is initially received by *modality-specific stores* (i.e. the sensory registers, which are specific stores for visual and auditory information) that hold information in a relatively uninterpreted form for very short periods of time (not more than a few seconds).

From the information bombarding the sensory stores, a small fraction is attended to and selected for further processing in the short-term memory. Information in the short-term memory is actively processed and may be transferred into the long-term memory during the time that it is being rehearsed in the short-term memory.

Forgetting involves different mechanisms in the three memory stores. Forgetting in the sensory registers occurs through spontaneous decay. In the short-term store there may be some decay, but forgetting is

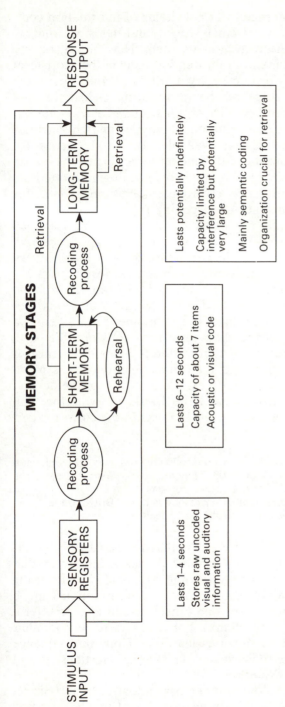

Figure 2.1   The multi-store or modal model of memory

caused primarily by interference from new items of information coming in. Short-term storage is extremely fragile and items are quickly lost once attention is diverted away from them. New inputs, or any kind of distraction, disrupt memory for items already in the short-term store. Forgetting in long-term memory is of two kinds. In *trace-dependent forgetting*, all trace of the information is lost; in *cue-dependent forgetting* the memory trace is still stored in the system but cannot be retrieved. Retrieval depends on employing the right retrieval cues and these cues are not always available. (In Part I, Section 6.4 described how subjects showed cue-dependent forgetting of the names of school-mates but recalled them successfully once they reinstated the right contextual cues. See Eysenck and Keane (1990), pp. 155–69, for a more detailed account of types of forgetting.)

In the multi-store or modal model Atkinson and Shiffrin described short-term memory in a way that conforms to our experience and intuitions, emphasizing its two main characteristics: (1) it has a very limited capacity; and (2) storage is easily disrupted. Most of us probably find it quite difficult to remember a seven- or eight-digit telephone number for the few seconds taken to dial it. The fact that people can hold in mind only seven or eight digits has sometimes been taken as a direct estimate of the size of the short-term memory store. Suppose, though, that you were asked to remember the following sequence of digits: '1066193911581815'. If you notice that the sequence is made up of the dates of the Battle of Hastings, the outbreak of the Second World War, the Spanish Armada, and the Battle of Waterloo, you could probably show perfect recall of all 16 digits in the correct order.

SAQ 6
Suppose several people were asked to learn the following sequence of numbers in the order given: 14 91 62 53 64 96 48 11 00. They are told to learn the sequence with (a) no hint; (b) the rule that the sequence consists of 1^2, 2^2, 3^2 up to 10^2; or (c) the information that the entire number corresponds to the British trade deficit in 1975. Which instruction should lead to the best recall?

How, then, can we make sense of the fact that the capacity of short-term memory appears to be very variable? A classic answer to that intriguing question was provided by George Miller (1956). Basically he argued that approximately seven *chunks* of information can be stored in short-term memory at any one time. It is not easy to offer a precise definition of the term 'chunk', but it refers to any familiar unit of information based on previous learning. Thus, the sequence '1066193915881815' can be reduced to four chunks: Hastings, World War II, Spanish Armada, Waterloo.

The Nobel-prize-winning economist and psychologist Herbert Simon (1974) tested George Miller's ideas in an experiment in which he was his own subject. He examined the capacity of short-term memory by measuring immediate memory span. This is a measure of how many items can be reported back in the right order straight after presentation, e.g. 7214568 or the words 'mind boy card egg ditto find'. Memory span for words and phrases was calculated in terms of syllables and words, and produced very variable estimates.

However, Simon argued that with lists of unrelated words each chunk would consist of an individual word, whereas with lists of phrases each phrase would form a single chunk. When he calculated the number of chunks on this basis, the data began to demonstrate some consistency, and suggested to Simon that the capacity of short-term memory is approximately five chunks.

Activity
You can investigate the notion that immediate recall is limited by the number of chunks by testing your own span, much as Simon did.
   Lists of two-word and eight-word phrases are given below.
1 Read each list aloud at approximately two words per second.
2 Immediately after each list, attempt to recall each phrase with the words in the correct order.
3 The span measure in chunks corresponds to the number of phrases recalled completely with words in the correct order.
If Simon is right in saying that a chunk corresponds to one phrase, the number of chunks forming the span measure should be similar for two-word and eight-word phrases, provided that they are all equally familiar.

Two-word phrases

Christmas Day	Pretty Polly
Football match	Good friends
Limited company	Coronation Street
Bank holiday	Closed shop

Eight-word phrases
I have nothing to declare except my genius
He goes by the name of King Creole
The evil that men do lives after them
Something is rotten in the state of Denmark
Curtsey while you are thinking what to say
Thus conscience doth make cowards of us all
What I tell you three times is true
Twopence a week, and jam every other day

Recent studies have shown that the number of items that can be stored and regurgitated can be expanded enormously if subjects are instructed in the use of chunking strategies and given very prolonged practice.

Kliegl and Baltes (1987) had subjects who could recall 120 digits. However these strategies take a considerable time to operate and the enlarged span which is demonstrated must therefore involve long-term memory as well as the short-term store. Without the use of elaborate and time-consuming strategies short-term memory capacity is small.

Why is short-term storage capacity so limited? Atkinson and Shiffrin claimed that there was a short-term store with a number of 'slots' into which chunks of information could be placed, and the limited capacity was due to the small number of slots. This view ascribes the limitations of short-term storage to *structural constraints*. But why should there be so few slots? Nowadays it is more usual to relate the limited capacity of short-term memory to *processing limitations*, in particular those associated with attention. There is strong evidence that our attentional processes are quite limited in terms of the number of things or events that can be attended to at any given moment. For example, if a dangerous situation develops while we are driving, our natural tendency is to stop talking in order to devote our limited attentional resources to the task of avoiding an accident.

In the newer theoretical approach, short-term memory is essentially synonymous with the allocation of attention, and a prime function of short-term memory is to concentrate on processing new inputs. Within this viewpoint, it seems natural that the limited capacity of attention should restrict the amount of information that can be held in short-term memory.

SAQ 7
The greater knowledge of adults means that they find chunking easier than children. Would you expect children or adults to be able to hold more items in short-term memory?

Summary of Section 1

- Memory involves the storage of information and its subsequent retrieval.
- In the Atkinson and Shiffrin model, short-term memory is regarded as one of a number of different kinds of memory store.
- The capacity of short-term memory has often been assessed by means of the memory span task (i.e. immediate recall of items in the correct order). One measure of capacity obtained from this task is based on the number of chunks recalled, where a chunk is a familiar unit or grouping of information.
- More recently, researchers consider that short-term memory capacity is limited by processing constraints (the allocation of attention), rather than by structural considerations (the amount of space available).

2   *Components of working memory*

Once short-term memory is seen as a mechanism for allocating attention it is clear that it is not just a passive repository for incoming
information. Instead, information is actively selected and actively
manipulated. We can choose whether to attend to people's faces, to an
unusual smell, or to the text of a book. When presented with information such as 'four times five equals nineteen', we can either simply
repeat it back to ourselves or engage in active processing and checking
of the information presented, thus discovering that the information is
false.

Baddeley and Hitch (1974) and Hitch and Baddeley (1976) were
impressed by this flexibility and diversity. It seemed intuitively obvious
to them that the short-term store is actively engaged in any cognitive
task which requires conscious thinking. Accordingly, they argued that
the concept of a short-term store serving simply as a temporary repository of information should be replaced with that of an active
working memory system with a functional role in a wide range of cognitive tasks. Secondly, they argued that working memory is a *complex
multi-component system* rather than a single unitary store. This working memory model has evolved out of a series of experiments in which
successive hypotheses about its structure and operation have been tested
and revised. The model as it is currently put forward (Baddeley, 1990)
is shown in Figure 2.2.

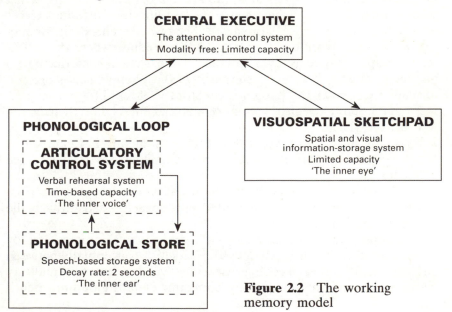

Figure 2.2   The working
memory model

The model includes three separate components: a modality-free *central executive*; a *phonological loop*; and a *visuospatial sketchpad*.

The *central executive* is a controlling attentional system which monitors and coordinates the operation of the other components, which are sometimes known as the slave systems. It is the most important element in the model since it is involved in any cognitively demanding task. It is called the 'central executive' because it allocates attention to inputs and directs the operation of the other components. The central executive has strictly limited capacity, and Baddeley suggested that 'the central executive is becoming increasingly like a pure attentional system' (1981a p. 22). In other words, the central executive is a very flexible system that can process information in any sensory modality in a variety of different ways. It can also store information over brief periods of time.

The *phonological loop* is itself subdivided into two separate components. The first of these is the *articulatory control system* which can hold information by articulating it subvocally. When we try to remember a telephone number by muttering it to ourselves we are using the articulatory control system. The articulatory control system is also used to hold the words we are preparing to speak aloud just before we actually utter them. It organizes information in a temporal and serial fashion, and can be regarded as the 'inner voice'. The second component is the *phonological store* which holds speech-based information in a phonological form and functions as an 'inner ear'. Memory traces held in the phonological store decay in about $1\frac{1}{2}$–2 seconds, but can be maintained by recycling items through the articulatory control system (that is, by subvocally rehearsing them) and feeding the refreshed traces back into the phonological store again. The two elements of the phonological loop also work together in tasks like reading, where the articulatory control system is used to convert the written material into a phonological code before registering it in the phonological store. Information can enter the phonological store in three different ways:
1 From the sensory register: auditory material enters directly from the sensory register.
2 From the articulatory control system: any material which is first subvocalized in the articulatory control system can feed into the phonological store.
3 From long-term memory: verbal information can be retrieved from long-term memory and represented in a speech-based form in the phonological store.

Both components of the phonological loop are considered to employ *phonological coding*. It is possible to distinguish conceptually between different levels of speech coding. An acoustic code is based on auditory features like pitch and loudness; a phonemic code is based on speech sounds like /b/ or /s/; and an articulatory code is based on the muscle movements necessary to produce the speech sounds. However, it is often difficult to distinguish between these levels of coding empirically. Baddeley has preferred to use the term 'phonological' in a sense which is neutral about the exact level of speech coding which is involved.

The *visuospatial sketchpad*, as its name implies, deals with visual and spatial information. It can receive inputs either directly from visual perception (via the visual sensory register) or by retrieving information from long-term memory in the form of images. At present it is unclear whether there is a single system which handles both visual and spatial information, or whether, as in the phonological loop, there are two separate subsystems, one for visual information and one for spatial information.

When might the visuospatial sketchpad be used in everyday life? One example is driving along a familiar road approaching a bend and thinking of the spatial layout of the road around the bend. This information is retrieved from long-term memory. Another example is seeing and remembering the handwriting on an envelope. Here the information has entered the visuospatial sketchpad from the sensory register. In both cases, the visuospatial sketchpad can be thought of as the 'inner eye'.

SAQ 8
Which components of the working memory system do you think might be involved in the following tasks?: (a) listening to a story; (b) remembering a telephone number; and (c) listening to instructions telling you how to get to a particular place.

You may be thinking by now that the working memory model provides an interesting way of theorizing about the various forms of active processing we engage in, but that it would be very difficult to test it. Although there is some truth in this view, Baddeley and Hitch did manage to develop a reasonably effective methodology for testing their model.

The basic approach involves asking people to perform two different tasks at the same time. These are known as *concurrent or interference tasks*. It is assumed that every component of the working memory system has a limited capacity to process information. The rationale is that, if two tasks make use of the same component or components of working memory, then performance of one or both tasks should be worse when they are performed together than when they are performed separately. Contrariwise, if the two tasks require different components of working memory, then it should be possible to perform them as well together as separately.

2.1 *The phonological loop*

We can see an example of this research strategy in operation in Techniques Box G. The issue is whether the articulatory control system in used in performing a memory span task. In this case, one of the concurrent tasks is designed to use the articulatory control system. A crucial assumption is that rapid repetition out loud of something mindless such as 'hi-ya' or 'the-the-the' uses up the resources of the articulatory control system so that it cannot be used for anything else. This technique is called *articulatory suppression*. It is difficult to know whether articulatory suppression totally knocks out the articulatory control system or whether it merely uses some of its resources. In either case, if the articulatory suppression results in poorer performance on another concurrent task, then it can be inferred that this second task also employs the articulatory control system. This experimental method of concurrent tasks is a general technique for exploring the components of working memory.

TECHNIQUES BOX G

Memory Span and Articulatory Suppression:
Wilding and Mohindra (1980)

Rationale
Wilding and Mohindra used the logic just described to investigate the involvement of the articulatory control system in memory span. They examined the effect of blocking the articulatory control system on performance of a concurrent task involving memory span for letter strings.

Method
Five letters were presented visually one after the other. All subjects received some *phonologically similar* letter strings like C D E P T (the letters all sound alike) and some *phonologically dissimilar* strings like H J M R Z (the letters sound different). After a short intervening task, subjects attempted to recall each sequence of five letters in the correct order. During presentation of the letters, subjects either performed an articulatory suppression task (saying 'the-the-the' continuously) or they had no additional task to perform (the no suppression condition).

Results
The probability of correctly recalling the 5-letter sequences in the various conditions is shown in Figure 2.3.

Interpretation
Several points emerge from these results. It is clear that, in the 'no suppression' condition, recall of phonologically similar strings is much

---

worse than recall of phonologically dissimilar strings. This finding, known as the *phonological similarity effect* indicates that both types of string are stored in the articulatory control system.

In the 'no suppression' condition the phonological loop functions normally. Because the loop uses a phonologically based system, this means that phonologically similar items get easily confused and are poorly recalled, but when the letters are phonologically dissimilar they are not confused and are recalled well.

With articulatory suppression, however, memory for similar and dissimilar items is equally poor. This is because the articulatory suppression task prevents the visually presented letters being converted by subvocalization into a phonological code. Hence the phonological characteristics of the letters exert no effect and there is no longer any superiority of the phonologically dissimilar items. This is known as the *articulatory suppression effect*.

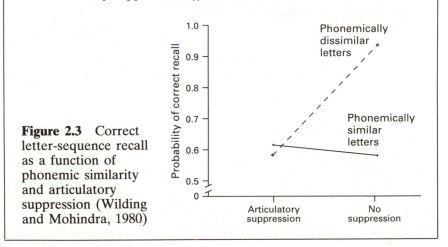

Figure 2.3 Correct letter-sequence recall as a function of phonemic similarity and articulatory suppression (Wilding and Mohindra, 1980)

The phonological similarity effect and the articulatory suppression effect both provide evidence for the phonological loop component of the working memory model. Additional information about the phonological loop was obtained in several experiments by Baddeley, Thomson, and Buchanan (1975). They discovered that the memory span performance for visually presented items was consistently better when short, one-syllable words (e.g. sum, hate) were presented than when the to-be-remembered list consisted of long, multi-syllable words (e.g. association, opportunity). This implied that the phonological loop could only hold a certain number of syllables. This so-called *word-length effect* only occurred if the articulatory control system was involved. If words were presented visually and the phonological loop was put out of action by articulatory suppression, then there was no effect of word length on span performance. Further experiments have shown conclusively that the crucial factor is not the number of syllables but the time it takes to say them. When a list consists of words with long-drawn-out vowels (like 'Friday', 'harpoon'), fewer of these are remembered than when a list consists of words which have the same number of syllables, but which are spoken more quickly (like 'cricket', 'bishop'). It has also been shown that digit span varies with the particular language being spoken and depends on the speed of articulation, so that digit span in Chinese (a rapidly spoken language) averages 9.9 items as compared with 6.6 for English and 5.8 for Welsh.

Both components of the phonological loop are involved in Baddeley's interpretation of the word-length effect. Items are held in the phonological store and their traces are refreshed by subvocalizing in the articulatory control system. With slower, longer words this recycling will take longer to complete and the traces of some items will decay before they can be refreshed. The results suggest that trace decay time is about two seconds. The memory span therefore depends both on how rapidly words can be subvocalized in the articulatory control system and how fast they decay in the phonological store. Any item has to be articulated at least once every two seconds if it is not to disappear from the store.

2.2 Visuospatial sketchpad

We have discussed the phonological loop component of working memory at some length, and yet it is clear that it is only of use when we need to hold verbal information in storage. Much of the time, the information that we want to make use of is in a non-verbal form, often being visual and/or spatial in character. In their attempt to accommodate this fact, Baddeley and Hitch postulated a visuospatial sketchpad (the 'inner eye').

TECHNIQUES BOX H

Spatial versus Visual Processing: Baddeley and Lieberman (1980)

Rationale
The functioning of the visuospatial sketchpad is more mysterious than that of the phonological loop, and it has proved difficult to identify its major characteristics. Baddeley and Lieberman made the important point that we should distinguish between spatial and visual processing. This distinction between spatial and visual processing may make more sense if we consider the position of people who have been blind since birth. Such people may possess accurate information about the spatial layout of objects in a room despite lacking any visual processing. Both spatial and visual processes may be involved in memory tasks.

Method

The memory task required the subject to imagine a 4×4 matrix. He or she was told that one particular square (the second square in the second row) was the starting square. The subject then heard a message that described the location of the digits 1 to 6 or 1 to 8 within the matrix and was asked to visualize each digit in its correct position. The digit 1 was always in the starting position, and then successive digits were placed in adjacent squares.

On some trials an easily visualized message was presented (e.g. 'in the starting square, put a 1; in the next square to the left, put a 2; in the next square down, put a 3' and so on). This message can be visualized as shown.

On other trials a nonsense message was presented. This was formally equivalent to the easily visualized message except that the words 'up' and 'down' were replaced by 'good' and 'bad', and the words 'left' and 'right' were replaced by 'slow' and 'quick' (e.g. 'in the starting square, put a 1; in the next square to the slow, put a 2; in the next square bad, put a 3' and so on). These nonsense messages have to be 'translated' before they can be visualized. The easily visualized messages contained 8 digits and the more difficult nonsense messages contained only 6 digits. It was established that this produced a comparable likelihood of correct reproduction of the matrix described by each kind of message.

In order to find out whether subjects used the visuospatial sketchpad with the easily visualized messages, Baddeley and Lieberman used the concurrent task technique. There were three conditions.

1 Message Only: subjects had the task of remembering either the easily visualized or nonsense messages, but there was no concurrent task.

2 Concurrent Visual Task: as well as remembering the messages, subjects did a concurrent visual task involving brightness judgements. Light patches were presented every 2.5 seconds and had to be judged bright or dim.

3 Concurrent Spatial Task: as well as remembering the messages subjects did a concurrent spatial task. Blindfolded subjects had to try to point a flashlight at a photocell located at the tip of a swinging pendulum. When they were successful, a bleep gave auditory feedback.

There were two groups of subjects: Group 1 did Conditions 1 and 2; Group 2 did Conditions 1 and 3.

	Mean number of correct reproductions (out of 8)	
Group 1		
Message	*Message only*	*With concurrent visual task*
Easily visualized	5.75	4.72
Nonsense	7.25	4.14
Groups 2		
Message	*Message only*	*With concurrent spatial task*
Easily visualized	6.75	3.14
Nonsense	6.50	5.14

Results
Statistical analysis showed that performance with the easily visualized messages was significantly impaired by the spatial task, whereas performance with the nonsense messages was disrupted by the visual task. None of the other differences was significant.

Interpretation
These findings clearly indicate that visual and spatial processes are functionally separate. In addition, as Baddeley and Lieberman pointed out, spatial processing appears to be more important than visual processing for retention of information presented in the form of easily visualized messages.

However, later experiments have suggested that there is a purely visual component (Baddeley, 1992). When subjects were given the task of learning word pairs using pictorial imagery it was found that passively looking at line drawings, or even colour patches, interfered with the imagery. In this case, a visual, but non-spatial, concurrent task impaired the ability to retain the visual images in the visuospatial sketchpad. Baddeley has now concluded that the visuospatial sketchpad is either one system with two separate dimensions, visual and spatial, or that it comprises two separate subsystems.

2.3   Central executive

The central executive is the most versatile of the components of the working memory system. It closely resembles attention, and thus possesses limited capacity, and it is of use in the active processing of information and in the transient storage of information. If we may assume that the central executive is involved in all attentionally-demanding tasks, then it follows that problem solving, reasoning, reading, mental arithmetic, learning, writing, and a host of other activities all utilize the central executive. The central executive is also involved in prospective memory, monitoring the performance of sequences of actions in the right order and at the right time. The slips of action described in Part I, Section 5.1 occur when the resources of the central executive have been diverted elsewhere.

Sometimes the involvement of the central executive is inferred from the fact that none of the other components of the working memory system appears to be involved. For example, in Techniques Box G we saw that a certain level of memory performance in a span task was possible even when the articulatory control system was largely suppressed. This suggests that the central executive may be involved in storage.

More direct evidence is available from comparing performance on two tasks that are performed either singly or together. This is known as the *dual-task technique*. The dual task technique is similar to the use of concurrent or interference tasks described earlier. However, the kind of concurrent task used to produce articulatory suppression is simply designed to cause interference, and the researcher is not interested in the level of performance on this muttering task. By contrast, with the dual-task technique, the researcher examines performance on *both* tasks and how each affects the other. With the dual-task technique, if the two tasks are very different but nevertheless interfere with each other, then it is plausible to assume that they are both competing for the same attentional resources of the limited capacity central executive. Hunt (1980) provided a good illustration of this technique. His subjects had to perform a psychomotor task and an intelligence test simultaneously. The psychomotor task was guiding a lever between two posts with the thumb and index finger of the left hand. The intelligence test was one known as Raven's Matrices, which involves reasoning about visual patterns. When both tasks were performed together, performance on the psychomotor task deteriorated progressively as the Raven problems became harder.

How should we interpret this interference effect? It seems highly unlikely that the two tasks both make use of any of the same specific processing systems (e.g. the phonological loop or the visuospatial sketchpad). Accordingly, the most plausible assumption is that they both make use of a very general processing system such as the central executive.

Baddeley now considers that the central executive is essentially similar to a model proposed by Norman and Shallice (1980) called the *Supervisory Attentional System (SAS)* which controls ongoing behaviour, maintaining goals and resisting distractions. Failures of the SAS to maintain control result in the slips of action discussed in Part I. Baddeley has also noted that performance of tasks which require the central executive are particularly impaired in Alzheimer's disease.

We have discussed the working memory model at some length. Of course, in order for the model to be of real use, we need to demonstrate that it can help to provide some understanding of the components involved in everyday activities such as reasoning and reading. It is to such issues that we now turn.

Summary of Section 2

- The working memory model replaces the unitary short-term store with four separate components: the central executive; the phonological loop which consists of two parts: an articulatory control system and a phonological store; and the visuospatial sketchpad.
- A major advantage of the working memory model is that it treats the short-term storage of information and more general processing activities within a single theoretical framework.
- If two tasks are performed at the same time, they should not interfere with each other if they make use of different components of the working memory system. In contrast, they should interfere if they both use one or more components in common. The most commonly used techniques are concurrent interference tasks like articulatory suppression and the dual-task technique.
- Some of the main experimental findings can be summarized as follows:
    (a) The phonological loop retains verbal information and can hold about two seconds' worth of syllables. It consists of a phonological store holding speech-based information and an articulatory control system which maintains information by subvocalization.
    (b) The visuospatial sketchpad appears to use spatial coding as well as or instead of visual coding.
    (c) The central executive is involved in all tasks that require attention.

3   Functions of working memory

An interesting question is how the resources of the working memory system are used in the performance of intellectually demanding tasks. It seems common sense to assume that such tasks would require close attention (and thus the resources of the central executive), but the involvement of the other components of the working memory system would presumably depend on the exact nature of the task.

SAQ 9
If you tried to solve visually presented anagrams, which component or components of working memory would probably be involved?

3.1   *Verbal reasoning problems*

A tasks that has been studied in some detail is the *verbal reasoning task* invented by Baddeley (1968). It consists of a series of short sentences, each of which is followed by two letters (A and B) either in the order 'AB' or 'BA'. Each sentence describes the order of the two letters (e.g. 'A precedes B'), and the subject's task is to decide as rapidly as possible whether the sentence is a true or a false description of the letter pair that follows it. The complexity of the task was varied by using different sentence forms.

Activity
Cover the page with a piece of card. Do each problem in turn, marking each one T (true) of F (false). If you have a stop watch you could try to keep a record of how long it takes you to solve each one. If you cannot time yourself, simply note which problems you found most difficult.
1 A precedes B: AB
2 B is preceded by A: BA
3 A does not follow B: BA
4 A is not followed by B: BA
5 B is not preceded by A: AB
6 A does not precede B: BA
7 B is followed by A: BA
8 B follows A: BA
When you have done that, check whether you have got all of the answers right: 1, 4, 6, and 7 are true, and 2, 3, 5, and 8 are false. Problems 1 and 8 use the active affirmative sentence form; problems 2 and 7 the passive affirmative; problems 3 and 6 the active negative; and problems 4 and 5 the passive negative. It is usually found that active affirmatives are the easiest, followed by passive affirmatives, active negatives, and passive negatives in that order. Is that what you found? If you managed to record times you probably found the times reflect the order of difficulty.

As you may have discovered when doing the verbal reasoning task, it seems necessary to use the attentional resources of the central executive to solve these problems, especially the more difficult ones. Since it is a verbal task, it is also possible that the phonological loop is involved. How can we decide whether or not the central executive and the phonological loop are involved in the performance of this task?

TECHNIQUES BOX I

Verbal Reasoning and Articulatory Suppression:
Hitch and Baddeley (1976)

Rationale

The basic strategy adopted by Hitch and Baddeley was to require their subjects to perform an additional concurrent interference task while performing the reasoning task. In Condition 1, the additional task was to say the word 'the' repeatedly, an articulatory suppression task assumed to involve only the articulatory control system. In Condition 2, the additional task was to say the sequence 'one two three four five six' over and over again. This number sequence is heavily overlearned, and so presumably it can be repeated automatically without requiring the attentional resources of the central executive. It was assumed therefore that this task would also involve only the articulatory control system. In Condition 3, the additional task was to repeat a different random string of six digits out loud on each trial, so this is equivalent to a memory-span task. In addition to using the articulatory control system, this task presumably required attention and thus involved the central executive. In Condition 4 (the control condition), no additional task was used. This condition provides a baseline against which to measure the detrimental effects (if any) on performance of the verbal reasoning task produced by the various additional tasks.

Method

Thirty-two versions of the problems in the verbal reasoning task were devised, comprising all possible combinations of sentence voice (active or passive), affirmation (affirmative or negative), truth value (true or false), verb (precedes or follows), and letter order. Each problem was presented visually, and during each trial the subject said 'the' repeatedly (Condition 1), or 'one two three four five six' (Condition 2), or repeated a string of six random digits (Condition 3), or there was no additional task (control condition). All subjects were run in all conditions. The time taken to press the 'True' or 'False' button was recorded.

Results

Speed of performance in the verbal reasoning task in each condition is shown in Figure 2.4.

The first point to note is that the performance was only slightly (and non-significantly) worse in the articulatory suppression conditions (i.e. Conditions 1 and 2: 'the' and 'one two three four five six') than

---

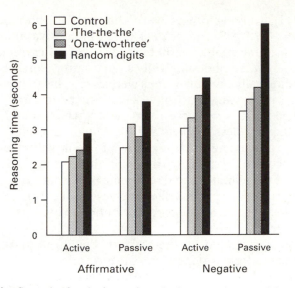

Figure 2.4   Speed of solution of verbal reasoning problems (Hitch and Baddeley, 1976)

in the control condition (4). This indicates that the articulatory control system plays little or no part in the performance of the verbal reasoning task. In contrast, the additional task that required use of the central executive as well as the articulatory control system (i.e. Condition 3: repeating a string of six random digits) produced a considerable increase in response time, especially with the more complex versions of the verbal reasoning task.

Interpretation
Hitch and Baddeley interpreted these results as demonstrating that the verbal reasoning task and the most demanding additional task (i.e. six random digits) both competed for the limited resources of the central executive, and it was this that slowed performance on the reasoning task. More complex versions of the verbal reasoning task presumably required more of the central executive's resources, and so were more adversely affected by the concurrent task.

You may have noticed from the figure that the data discussed above suggest that articulatory suppression might have been affecting verbal reasoning slightly, even though the effects were non-significant. Hitch and Baddeley (1976) further explored the possible involvement of the articulatory control system in verbal reasoning in another experiment. They used the same verbal reasoning task that has already been described, but this time they varied the letter pairs. Some of the letter pairs were composed of phonemically similar (sound-alike) letters (BP;

MN; FS; TD), whereas others were composed of phonologically dissimilar letters (MC; VS; OQ; XY). The key finding was that the number of verbal reasoning problems that could be solved correctly in a given time was lower when phonologically similar letter pairs were used than when phonologically dissimilar ones were used. This indicates that some phonological processing must have been occurring during the reasoning task since there is no reason why letters which sound alike should be more difficult unless subjects are sounding them out to themselves. Phonological processing has been shown to be largely a function of the articulatory control system, so it seems that the articulatory control system is used to facilitate verbal reasoning performance. In other words, while verbal reasoning primarily involves the central executive, it is likely that there is also a modest contribution made by the articulatory control system.

We have concentrated on the ways in which the performance of a verbal reasoning task is dependent on the various components of the working memory system. The general conclusion from the research discussed so far is that it is relatively straightforward to discover which components of working memory are involved in reasoning or other cognitively taxing tasks. By seeing which additional, concurrent tasks impair performance on the main task, we can build up a picture of how that task is normally approached.

As you have undoubtedly discovered already, psychology has been noted throughout its history for theoretical controversies. There are various theorists who object to the notion that there is a general, modality-free system such as the central executive which can direct attention to the needs of various tasks. They would therefore dispute the interpretation just given of the factors responsible for verbal reasoning performance. According to Allport (1980), the term 'attention' (and, thus, also 'central executive') is used in a rather vague way without any adequate specification of how it actually functions. This vagueness means that it can be used to explain almost any experimental results that are found. When two cognitively demanding tasks are performed together, disruption of performance can be 'explained' in terms of exceeding the capacity of attention or the central executive; but when there is no disruption this too can be accounted for by assuming that the two tasks do not exceed the available resources of the central executive. This line of argument, which is to be found in the article by Hitch and Baddeley (1976), is suggestive of 'Heads I win, tails you lose' and runs the danger of becoming entirely circular. Furthermore, since explanations based on the central executive are all too easy to provide, they may have the disadvantage of preventing us from examining in detail what is happening.

It is probably fair to state that Baddeley and Hitch would agree that relatively little is known of the workings of the central executive or attentional system. However, the fact that very different tasks often cause interference with each other (as in Hunt's dual-task experiment) suggests the existence of some very general processing resource such as attention or the central executive. Furthermore, theories in psychology are typically only abandoned when better theories are proposed, and it is not clear that this point has been reached as yet.

Summary of Section 3.1

- Verbal reasoning primarily involves the central executive, but may also involve the phonological loop to some extent.
- There is controversy concerning the usefulness of the theoretical construct of the central executive and its role in directing attention.

3.2 Working memory and reading

Over the years there has been much interest in the processes involved in reading. A controversy that continues to this day concerns the role (if any) played by subvocalization in reading. Some powerful arguments in favour of the view that reading depends on inner speech or the articulatory control system were put forward by Huey (1908) in his classic text, *The Psychology and Pedagogy of Reading*:

> The carrying range of inner speech is considerably larger than that of vision ... the initial subvocalization seems to help hold the word in consciousness until enough others are given to combine with it in touching off the unitary utterance of the sentence which they form ... It is of the greatest service to the reader or listener that at each moment a considerable amount of what is happening should hang suspended in the primary memory of the inner speech. (Huey, 1908, pp. 144–8).

Although the terminology used by Huey may have a somewhat dated air about it, the gist of what he has to say has a surprisingly modern feel. The fact that it is called inner speech appears to equate it with the articulatory control system, the inner voice where words are sounded out and prepared for speech. However, it is possible that the phonological store or inner ear is also involved in the transient storage of sentence information for subsequent use.

It will perhaps come as no surprise to learn that the involvement of the articulatory control system in reading seems to depend on the nature of the reading task. After all, reading a popular novel for pleasure is a very different activity from inspecting the small print of a legal contract. Intuition suggests that we are more likely to resort to subvocalization when what we are reading is complicated, and this was confirmed in an ingenious study by Hardyck and Petrinovich (1970). They found that people tend to show increased muscle activity of the larynx when they are reading. When they trained their subjects to suppress this muscle activity while reading, there was no effect on comprehension of simple prose passages, but comprehension of complex prose suffered.

It is of particular interest to consider the effect of articulatory suppression on reading. According to the normal concurrent task rationale, if suppression of the articulatory control system does *not* hinder reading, this implies that the control system is not used in reading. Sometimes the effects of articulatory suppression are negligible or nonexistent. The task of deciding whether simple sentences (e.g. *Canaries have wings*) are true or false was performed as rapidly and accurately with articulatory suppression as without it (Baddeley, 1979). However, there may be some doubts as to whether this is a proper reading task because of its simplicity. Levy (1978) investigated some of the factors determining whether or not the articulatory control system is used in reading. She discovered that reading to extract the gist was not affected by articulatory suppression. However, when subjects had to remember the exact wording of visually presented sentences, there was a detrimental effect of articulatory suppression on performance.

Baddeley, Eldridge and Lewis (1981) also made use of articulatory suppression. They used sentences which were either meaningful or anomalous. An example of an anomalous sentence is: *She doesn't mind going to the dentist to have fillings, but doesn't like the rent when he gives her the injection at the beginning.* Subjects had to decide whether each sentence was meaningful or anomalous, a task that requires close attention to the individual words. Performance was adversely affected by articulatory suppression.

How can we explain the fact that in some reading tasks saying 'the-the-the' (articulatory suppression) has an interfering effect, but in others it does not? While we do not have a complete answer as yet, it appears that the articulatory control system tends to be used when the central executive is becoming overloaded. This is a possible explanation of the effects on reading complex prose material noted by Hardyck and Petrinovich (1970) and on the difficult task of distinguishing between meaningful and anomalous sentences (Baddeley, Eldridge and Lewis, 1981). Since the articulatory control system seems to be particularly useful at preserving the order in which verbal items are presented, it is only to be expected that it is used when the reading task requires word-for-word recall (Levy, 1978).

If the articulatory control system does play a significant role in reading, the next issue is to consider exactly how it facilitates reading. The most popular view, expressed in the quotation from Huey (1908) given above, is that the intake of visual information from the printed page leads to a verbatim record of the last few words in the articulatory control system and this record is then used in the comprehension process. There is increasing evidence that this view is profoundly mistaken, in part because it implies that comprehension is a rather slow and laborious process. Contrary evidence was obtained by Rayner, Carlson, and Frazier (1983) using measurements of eye movements. They asked people to read a sentence such as: *As she was sewing the sleeve fell off her lap.* While readers initially assumed that the subject of the sentence was the person doing the sewing rather than the sleeve, they corrected their error very quickly, as revealed by the fact that the word 'fell' was fixated for an abnormally long time. This means that the inaccurate first interpretation was detected quickly enough to affect eye movements occurring within approximately 250 milliseconds. Clearly, comprehension is not delayed until after subvocalization has taken place.

The most obvious problem with the notion that reading involves a sequential process of visual information intake, followed by recoding as a phonological representation in the articulatory control system, and finally comprehension, is that it seems to imply that the articulatory control system always forms a vital part of the reading process. This is, of course, refuted by the various studies in which articulatory suppression had no effect at all on reading. Perhaps the articulatory control system acts as a kind of back-up system that is used as and when a current reading task becomes too difficult for whatever reason. If the reading task is straightforward and easy, the visual information may be comprehended directly without utilizing the articulatory control system.

These conclusions have been confirmed by studies of brain-damaged patients with greatly reduced short-term memory spans. A patient has been reported whose digit span was only two items, indicating that the articulatory control system was severely impaired. Nevertheless, she could read and understand six word sentences, and even longer ones provided that accurate retention of the precise word order was not essential for comprehension. This case study shows that some reading comprehension is possible when the articulatory control system only functions very poorly. However, in normal people there is a strong association between working memory span and reading, such that people with a high working memory span show better comprehension (Baddeley, 1990, pp. 136–41).

It is natural to wonder why the emphasis in this section on the use of working memory in reading has been so heavily on the articulatory control system component of the working memory system, especially since common sense indicates that the central executive, the visuospatial sketchpad, and the phonological store may all play a part in normal reading. The reason is simply that, because convenient techniques exist, nearly all of the research has investigated the articulatory control system. It is especially unfortunate that so little is known of the role of the central executive and the other components, but these are more difficult to investigate.

Summary of Section 3.2

- Inner speech is sometimes (but not invariably) used in reading.
- Inner speech is represented in the articulatory control system, which is most likely to be used in reading when the text material is difficult and/or when the exact order in which verbal items are represented must be remembered.
- The evidence suggests that the articulatory loop does not constitute a vital component of the reading process; rather, it acts as a back-up system.

3.3   An evaluation of working memory

Baddeley's working memory model represents a valuable contribution in various ways. There is by now almost universal agreement that it is much more realistic to assume that working memory consists of several relatively independent processing mechanisms rather than a single unitary short-term store. It also seems useful to treat attentional processes and short-term storage as parts of the same system, primarily because they are probably used together much of the time in everyday life. Finally, the notion that any one component of the working memory system may be involved in the performance of a great number of apparently very different tasks is a valuable insight. The best illustration of this notion is the articulatory control system, which has been shown to be used in memory span tasks and mental arithmetic, and, to a lesser extent, in verbal reasoning and reading.

Perhaps the greatest limitation of the working memory model is that we know least about the component that is undoubtedly of greatest general importance, the central executive. The central executive is presumably used to deal with the demands of ongoing tasks or activities, allocating attention to various aspects of the tasks, and integrating and evaluating results, but we know very little about how this is achieved.

In spite of the frequent assertions by Baddeley and Hitch that one of the major characteristics of the central executive is its limited capacity, there have never been any successful attempts to measure that capacity. A further difficulty with the central executive has been raised by Richardson (1984). He pointed out the way in which the central executive can apparently carry out an enormous variety of processing activities of different kinds. This variety poses obvious problems in terms of describing the precise function of the central executive and may indicate that the notion of a single central executive is as misplaced as the idea of a unitary short-term memory. Allport (1980) and others have suggested replacing a central allocation of attention with several specific processing mechanisms. Perhaps surprisingly, Baddeley (1981b) has himself argued for a somewhat similar position. He argued that his strategy was to identify as many specific processing mechanisms as possible (e.g. the articulatory control system, and the visuospatial sketchpad), thus progressively chipping away at the central executive. According to this view, the central executive can be thought of as the remaining area of ignorance.

However, there are good reasons why we should not abandon the notion of some general central executive. If the human mind really consisted of nothing but numerous specific processing mechanisms operating in isolation from each other, it seems likely that total chaos would result. At the very least, some central system seems to be needed in order to coordinate the activities of the specific mechanisms, and the central executive seems well suited to that role.

A major limitation of the working memory model is that it has very little to say about the changes in strategy that occur over time as a result of practice. For example, we all know that driving a car is extraordinarily demanding for a learner driver, but relatively effortless for an experienced one. In the same way, expert mathematicians might be able to perform effortlessly mental calculations that would be almost impossible for other people to do. Of course, this change can be described in terms of a reduction in the use of the attentional resources of the central executive with practice, but this does not even begin to explain what has happened.

In this connection, a useful distinction (introduced in Part I, Section 5.1) has been suggested between attentional processing, which requires conscious control, and automatic processing. There has been a certain amount of disagreement about the defining criteria for automatic processing, but the main criteria adopted (LaBerge, 1981) include the following. Automatic processes:

1 occur without awareness;
2 are highly efficient;
3 have no capacity limitations;
4 are difficult to modify;
5 are involuntary.

It appears that well-learned complex tasks can sometimes become automatic and can be performed without making any use of the resources of working memory. Of course, substantial amounts of practice are typically needed to achieve automaticity, and automaticity only develops when task demands are relatively invariant.

Finally, it is likely that the working memory system can be used even more flexibly than has generally been assumed. In particular, it is unwise to assume that the components of working memory used in the performance of a given task are always the same. For example, it has often been assumed that memory span for digits involves the articulatory control system, and, as predicted, articulatory suppression reduces digit span. Suppose we gave people massive practice at the digit-span task under articulatory suppression conditions. Is it not likely that they would develop some alternative strategy for performing the digit-span task without using the articulatory control system?

The model of production systems which follows in Part IIB sheds some light on these issues.

Further reading

BADDELEY, A.D. (1990) *Human Memory: Theory and Practice*, Lawrence Erlbaum Associates. This is a very comprehensive and up-to-date account of research in memory.

EYSENCK, M.W. and KEANE, M.T. (1990) *Cognitive Psychology: A Student's Handbook*, Lawrence Erlbaum Associates. Chapters 5 and 6 on memory include both experimental and clinical work.

ROTH, I. (ed.) (1990) *Introduction to Psychology: Volume 2*, Lawrence Erlbaum Associates and The Open University. Chapter 12 on memory gives a more detailed account of the modal or multi-store model and criticisms of it.

Part IIB
Memory Systems:
The Computer Modelling
Approach

George Kiss

Contents

1   Memory systems in computer models of cognition

1.1   Programs as psychological models

The construction of computer models has been widely used by psychologists as a method of both formulating and testing their theories. Theories about memory are no exception. Part IIA looked at psychological models of memory that have been formulated and tested through *experimentation*. In Part IIB we shall look at some models of memory that have been formulated and tested as *computer programs*. Since the whole of Part II of this book is concerned with memory *systems*, it is very appropriate that we should take a broader view of how a more comprehensive and general theory of cognition makes use of them.

Look back at Figure 2.1 in Part IIA which shows the so-called 'multistore' or 'modal' model of memory. This model of memory distinguishes several component parts, some of which are structures (sensory registers, short-term memory, long-term memory), while others are processes (coding, rehearsal, retrieval). Such a diagram might be regarded as a blueprint describing the overall structure and functioning of memory, made up from some major components, like short-term memory, etc. Diagrams or blueprints of this kind are often said to represent the *architecture* of a system. They show the organization of a complex system without getting lost in the finer details. So Figure 2.1 is an architecture for human memory, derived from many years of experimental research in psychology.

Figure 2.5 (on p. 96) shows an even more general diagram that attempts to represent the whole of human cognitive architecture in terms of a few large components. We shall look at the question of how memory components fit into such an architecture. But first let us fill in a little history about the origin of the theories that led to the construction of such architectures.

2   General models of cognition

In recent years several cognitive psychologists have become dissatisfied with the piecemeal theorizing that is so prevalent in experimental psychology. They are attempting to return to theorizing on a larger scale, more in the style of the 'grand theories' that were constructed in the early stages of the history of psychology, for example by William McDougall and William James.

There are two good examples of this. One is work by Allen Newell's group on a system called SOAR, the other is John Anderson's work on a system called ACT* (which stands for Adaptive Control of Thought). Both of these projects constitute extensive research programmes which have been going on for several years. They are aimed at the construction of comprehensive models of cognition, using a relatively small set of components (Newell, 1989).

Interestingly, both models give major emphasis to a variety of memory systems as components of the overall cognitive architecture. For this reason, the ACT* model will be described in some detail in this chapter. However, keep in mind that the scope of the ACT* model is considerably broader than just memory, as it has been used as the basis for simulations of problem-solving behaviour, the learning of skills, language understanding and acquisition, and memory retrieval (Anderson, 1976, 1983). Nor is ACT* a finished and fixed system. Anderson and his collaborators have produced a whole evolutionary series of models of which ACT* is just one. The model preceding ACT* was HAM and the one suceeding it is called PUPS. ACT* itself is a member of a series of ACT models. You see, the theoretician's work is never 'done'! The best we can do is to take a snapshot of this ongoing enterprise. We have selected ACT* because a considerable amount of effort has been spent on exploring its usefulness in accounting for psychological phenomena and findings, which is not yet the case with the more recent models. Part IIB will concentrate on this work, emphasizing its relevance to theorizing about memory systems.

Both Newell and Anderson have argued that there is a single computational device, called a *production system*, which is so general and versatile that it provides the perfect medium for building general cognitive models. This idea was first proposed by Newell (1973) and later implemented in the SOAR system (Laird, Newell and Rosenbloom, 1987). Anderson's (1983) ACT* system also uses a production system as a major component. In order to understand how ACT* works, you will need to know what production systems are. We therefore start by looking at the concept of a production system in Techniques Box J. You should now study this and then answer SAQ 10.

SAQ 10
In order to test your understanding of production systems, modify the production system shown in Techniques Box J so that it will also cope with the situation when you run out of tea instead of milk. How could you do this without having to duplicate all three productions? State what rules have to be added and which rule(s) modified and how. (Hint: make rule 2 more general!)

TECHNIQUES BOX J

Production Systems

All production system models of cognition are based on the idea that knowledge is represented in long-term memory in the form of *condition/action rules*. Each of these rules, called *productions*, specifies the exact conditions in which an action should take place.

For instance, if you see flames coming out of an office, this is the *condition* for the *action* of shouting 'Fire'. The general notion is that behaviour is a response to a current situation. The situation is first recognized and then appropriate action is taken. A *production system* consists of a set of production rules, a working memory and a cyclic *recognize–act* process. Here is a simple set of productions:

Production rule 1
Condition: IF your goal is to make a cup of tea but you have no milk
Action: THEN activate a goal of buying milk

Production rule 2
Condition: IF your goal is to buy milk and you have enough money
Action: THEN go to the shop

Production rule 3
Condition: IF you are in the shop and your goal is to buy milk
Action: THEN say 'A pint of milk please'

Note that the condition part of Production 2 would fail if you have no money, and that this miniature production rule set does not provide any way to overcome that difficulty. You should find it easy to add some rules to cope with this impasse.

The recognize–act cycle is responsible for selecting which rule is applicable by comparing the condition parts of the rules to the contents of the working memory and carrying out the actions if there is a match. If there are several applicable production rules, the conflict has to be resolved by using some *conflict resolution* principles. We shall not discuss these principles in detail here, but an example of such a principle would be to choose the rule which has not been used recently.

The actions may refer to external actions, like 'Go to the shop', or to internal actions, like 'Activate the goal of buying milk'. Often the action part of a production is to add new information to the working memory. Activating a goal is done in this way too.

Production systems are like the S–R associations of classical learning theory. The 'IF' part of a rule is like the 'stimulus' part of an S–R pair; the 'THEN' part is like the 'response'.

3   *The ACT* system*

The ACT* system architecture consists of three memories: *working memory*, *declarative memory* and *procedural memory*, as shown in Figure 2.5. Each of these components will be discussed in detail in the next few sections, but here are some hints on how you could think about them in terms of concepts that you already know.

The concept of working memory is already familiar to you from Section 2 of Part IIA.

Declarative and procedural memory are both types of long-term memory, which has also been mentioned in Part IIA. Together, declarative and procedural memory constitute the stored *knowledge* used by the system.

Declarative memory contains knowledge stored by means of a variety of different kinds of *representations* that you can think of as schemas of the kind described in Section 3.2 of Part I.

Procedural memory contains knowledge about *actions* linked to conditions. The linking is done in the form of productions, as was

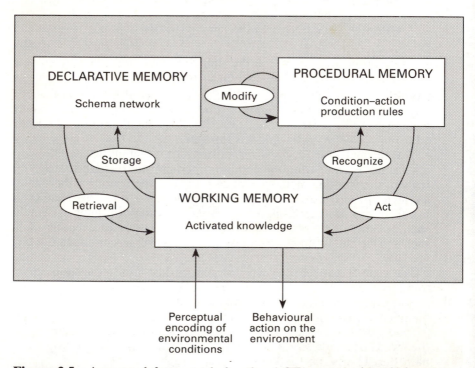

Figure 2.5   A general framework for the ACT* system, identifying the major structural components and their interlinking processes (adapted from Anderson, 1983)

shown in Productions 1, 2 and 3 in Techniques Box J. You can relate the concept of condition–action pairs to the contents of Section 5 in Part I, which discussed how memory relates to our *actions*, especially our slips of action, and to the idea of prospective memory (i.e. remembering to *act* when the *conditions* are right).

There are some similarities between the 'multi-store' or 'modal' model described in Section 2 of Part IIA and the ACT* model. You might like to compare Figure 2.5 to Figure 2.1 in Part IIA. As you will see in more detail in a moment, the ACT* model adds to and extends the multi-store model, particularly by being more explicit about the nature of the processes connecting the boxes in that model. These processes are the storage and retrieval processes transferring information between working memory and declarative memory; and the recognize and act processes operating between procedural memory and working memory.

The basic framework embodies a fundamental assumption which is that the system stores two different types of knowledge: declarative and procedural. Declarative knowledge corresponds to facts, or statements, such as 'Paris is the capital of France', or 'John gave the book to Mary'. Procedural knowledge, on the other hand, corresponds to the knowledge underlying our ability to do things: for example, the procedural knowledge of how to ride a bicycle. It is a general finding that facts are relatively easy to commit to memory, whereas new procedures can generally only be created after much practice. The distinction reflects the fact that there are two ways of knowing: *knowing that* (declarative) and *knowing how* (procedural). One is just information, the other links information to action.

SAQ 11
Assuming that you know them, classify each of the following items as being declarative or procedural knowledge from your own personal point of view:
1 President Kennedy is dead.
2 To make tea, boil some water, pour it over a tea bag and let it stand for three minutes.
3 If you can't stand the heat, get out of the kitchen.
4 The quick brown fox jumped over the lazy dog.
5 2 + 2 = 4.

During the operation of the ACT* system, seven kinds of processes take place:
1 *Encoding processes* lay down information about the current state of the external world in working memory. These representations are the output of the perceptual system.
2 *Storage processes* create new permanent records in (long-term) declarative memory from the knowledge structures stored in working memory and may also augment the strength of existing knowledge

structures. The strength depends on how often the knowledge structure has been used.

3 *Retrieval processes* access information in declarative memory and place it in working memory; that is, they make it active.

4 *A recognition (matching) process* compares all the data active in working memory with the condition parts of all the production rules stored in procedural memory. Taking the example in Techniques Box J, if the working memory contains 'your goal is to buy milk', this will match part of the condition of Rule 2: IF 'your goal is to buy milk . . .'.

5 *The action process* deposits the structures produced by the matched production rules into working memory. Continuing with our example, if activated, Rule 1 would deposit a goal of buying milk into working memory.

6 *Performance processes* transform commands temporarily stored in working memory into behavioural action. These processes correspond to the functions of motor systems. In our example, 'go to the shop' would be executed as such a behavioural action.

7 *Modification processes* create new productions through monitoring the application of existing productions. They are involved in the modelling of learning, with which we shall not be concerned in this book.

Let us now look at the component memory systems in more detail.

3.1   Working memory

Working memory has a central role within the architecture. It contains the information the system can currently access. This includes information retrieved from long-term declarative memory, temporary knowledge structures deposited by perceptual processes encoding the current situation, and any other structures added to working memory by the actions of production rules. Essentially, working memory embraces all items of declarative knowledge, permanent or temporary, which are in an active state. (We shall discuss, in Section 3.2, how this active state is produced). The working memory used in ACT* is very similar to the working memory outlined in earlier sections of Part IIA of this book. Working memory takes part in all but the last of the seven processes listed above.

3.2   Declarative memory

Declarative memory stores three types of knowledge representation:

> *temporal strings* which encode primarily sequence information (e.g. Monday, Tuesday, Wednesday, . . .);

spatial images which encode configural information (e.g. a triangle above a square);

abstract propositions which encode semantic information that can form the content of sentences of a language. For example, (HATE [Bill, Fred]) would express the contents of the sentence 'Bill hates Fred'.

These different representational types facilitate different forms of cognitive processing. For example, judgements of serial order are easier when based on the processing of information encoded as strings; determining the relative positions of objects in a remembered scene is facilitated by the processing of spatial images; while the making of inferences in reasoning is more suited to the processing of abstract propositions. Different aspects of cognition involve different types of processing which are made efficient by encoding the requisite information in the most compatible format.

All three forms of knowledge structure are interconnected to form a single declarative network structure. An example is shown in Figure 2.6. This example shows how declarative knowledge about having a meal in a restaurant might be represented. Anderson calls this kind of structure a *tangled hierarchy*. Such a structure is tangled because the connecting arrows do not form a neat tree-like structure, but criss-cross arbitrarily between the nodes. It is also hierarchical, in the sense that information is successively expanded into more and more detail as we move downwards in the diagram.

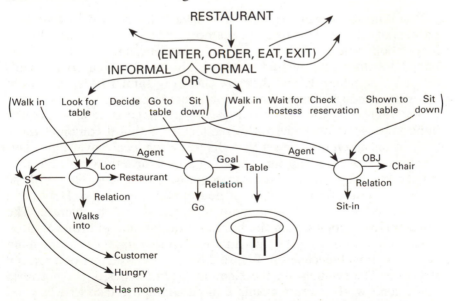

Figure 2.6   An example of a tangled hierarchy stored in declarative memory (adapted from Anderson, 1983)

Although the diagram looks a bit confusing at first sight, think of it as a network consisting of nodes and connecting lines. For example, ENTER is a node, the string (Walk in, Look for table, Decide, Go to table, Sit down) is also a node, and so is each oval shape (a proposition), as is the little picture of a table (a spatial image). Thus, in this type of network *a node can represent a string, a proposition, an element of one of these, or a spatial image.* The connecting arrows are sometimes labelled by the name of the relationship holding between the nodes connected by the arrow. For example, within the representation of the proposition 'S walks into a restaurant' on the left-hand side of Figure 2.6, we find the 'Loc' label over an arrow connecting the oval to 'Restaurant', indicating that the relationship is one of location. Compare this figure with Figure 1.4 in Part I, showing a 'picnic schema'. You can see that the picnic schema also represents the location of a picnic, this time by using the slot labelled PLACE which contains the value OUTDOORS. Although the diagrammatic tools used in these two diagrams are different, the content is the same: there is a *relation* which connects two objects. This is how this works:

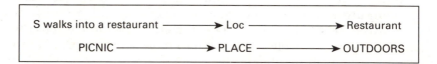

You will also recall that schemas have been defined in Part I as packets of information stored in memory, representing general knowledge about objects, situations, events or actions, and that they can be linked together into related systems. This is also what Anderson's tangled hierarchies do and they are therefore similar to the notion of schemas, although they are more elaborate structures.

The representations discussed so far are *static* structures. A very important aspect of Anderson's architecture is that it combines these with an *activation* mechanism that changes *dynamically* over time. This combination was a major innovation in Anderson's theorizing because it linked two separate traditions in cognitive psychology. One of these traditions comes from the work of neuropsychologists, like Hebb, and uses *activation patterns* as the main representational mechanism. The other tradition comes from the influence of the field of artificial intelligence on cognitive psychology, and uses *symbol structures* as the main representational mechanism. Figure 2.6 is a good example of a symbol structure. The symbols are the elements at the nodes of the network. Anderson's work is a rare example of an attempt to take what is good from both ideas and to combine them in a single architecture.

This is significant in relation to the current debate between the proponents of artificial intelligence models like ACT* on the one hand, and parallel distributed processing (PDP) models on the other hand (we shall be looking at such models in detail in Part III of this book). The PDP models also use activation patterns as the main representational mechanism.

In ACT*, the declarative memory network functions as a *spreading activation mechanism*. What this means is that activation circulates around the network; different nodes have different levels of activation at any particular instant in time. The most active nodes within declarative memory become the content of working memory. In this way, the spreading activation is used as an information retrieval mechanism. Associated with each node in the declarative memory network there is also a strength value which reflects the frequency of use of the conceptual item represented by the node. The relative strengths of nodes determine the amount of activation that flows down the links that connect them. The strength values of the nodes therefore play a part in determining the distribution of activation over the network.

Activation is injected into the network through *source nodes*, which are thus the nodes where activation originates and spreads over the network. There are three ways in which a node can become a source node: through perceptual input; through activation by a production rule; and through activation as a goal structure. We shall now discuss these briefly.

1 *Perceptual source nodes* provide a constant source of activation as long as the corresponding perceptual stimulus is maintained. As an example of a perceptual source node, imagine that the words *dog* and *chair* are used in a memory experiment on paired-associate learning. Figure 2.7 shows a spreading activation network that surrounds these words after the learning stage has been completed, and indicates how activation may spread when the word *dog* is presented as a retrieval cue in the test stage of the experiment. While the subject is focusing attention on *dog*, the node representing the cor-

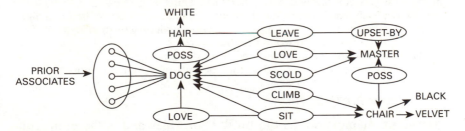

Figure 2.7   The spread of activation in the neighbourhood of the paired associates *dog-chair*, after the retrieval cue *dog* has been presented (adapted from Anderson, 1983)

101

responding word is constantly activating its neighbours in declarative memory.

2 *Source nodes activated by production rules.* We said when discussing the kinds of processing that take place during the operation of the ACT* system that what production rules do is to deposit knowledge structures into working memory. What actually happens in ACT* is that the relevant knowledge structures are made into temporary source nodes. They are temporary because the activation begins to decay as soon as the associated production rule actions are complete.

3 *Source nodes associated with goal structures* (which we shall describe in more detail in section 3.4) differ in that they can be maintained without decay; this allows the system to make use of goal-directed processing.

Working memory, as indicated in Section 3.1, corresponds to those regions of declarative memory that are most active. As a possibly useful analogy, think of the state of activation as a mountainous landscape; the higher the activation, the greater the height of the landscape. Now assume that a threshold height is fixed by the designer of ACT*. Then any declarative memory element that has an activation above this threshold height, up to the height of the mountain peaks, will correspond to the contents of working memory. The mountain peaks will usually correspond to source nodes and will be surrounded by regions of high activation that form each mountain.

Working memory contains both temporary structures and permanent declarative structures which are temporarily highly active. For any temporary structure stored in working memory, there is a given probability that it will be made a permanent declarative memory structure. Declarative structures created in this way are initially given a minimum strength value, but if the created knowledge structure already exists in long-term memory then its strength is increased.

SAQ 12
The spreading activation mechanism can be thought of as sending messages or information between the nodes of a network. Think of an analogy in which the network is a telephone network and the nodes are homes with a telephone installed. Activation corresponds to receiving a call. The strength of activation is the number of calls received per day. Now answer the following:
1 What does a source node correspond to in this analogy?
2 Which homes would correspond to the contents of working memory?

3.3 Procedural memory

Procedural memory stores the production rules and is therefore concerned with actions. Anderson calls it the production memory. However, I shall continue to call it procedural memory to emphasize the contrast with declarative memory.

The interface between procedural memory and working memory is the recognize phase of the recognize–act cycle. Pattern recognition is the essence of this phase. *Pattern matching* is the mechanism that recognizes which production rules apply when. As we have seen in Techniques Box J, rule selection is achieved by matching the contents of working memory against the condition parts of all the production rules stored in procedural memory. Given the number of such rules, it is obviously necessary for the mechanism to employ some form of parallel matching process.

It is widely realized in psychology that pattern matching is a fundamental component of many aspects of cognition. It underlies most of the problems relating to visual and acoustic perception, and is an important aspect of language comprehension. Moreover, it seems to be involved in the retrieval from memory of appropriate schemas and strategies during problem solving, particularly when analogies between problems are involved. In ACT* too, pattern matching has a key role, since it is only through matching the contents of working memory with production rule conditions that internal processing can function.

The pattern matching mechanism used by Anderson allows partial matching when complete matches are not found for any of the rules. As long as a production rule's condition provides the best match to the available data, and the condition pattern is sufficiently activated (that is, above some specified minimum level), then the production rule will apply. For example, working memory may contain the information *your goal is to make a mug of tea*, and procedural memory may contain two relevant production rules:

P1: IF your goal is to make a drink
    THEN ...

P2: IF your goal is to make a cup of tea
    THEN ...

Neither of the rules matches the contents of working memory exactly, but the condition part of P2 provides a closer match than P1, and may be activated sufficiently for it to be applied.

Anderson makes use of this property in explaining certain errors in skilled performance. For example, it may be used to explain some of the slips of action mentioned in Part I of this book (Reason's slips of action), like pouring hot water from the kettle into the sugar bowl instead of the teapot. Perhaps the relevant pattern only specifies 'Pour the water into the container', and the best match to the container happens to be the sugar bowl because of its position on the table. Explanations of this kind are helped by another aspect of Anderson's matching mechanism. The matcher is sensitive to activation levels and will try harder to match elements that have high activation levels. This might explain some of the slips of action described in Part I, where 'strong habits' intrude inappropriately into an action sequence.

Pattern matching the contents of working memory against production rule conditions is a fundamental component of all production systems. Moreover, it is the most expensive component of such systems in terms of the amount of processing it involves: even the most efficient pattern matcher soaks up 95 per cent of the processing time in a working production system computer simulation. If production systems were a valid model of human cognition, this would imply that pattern matching should be the major processing bottleneck in human cognition too. This does not seem to be the case — humans are extremely good at pattern matching, as shown by their performance in recognizing handwriting, faces, and objects of all kinds. The reason may be that the human architecture uses specialized parallel distributed processing systems for pattern matching. We shall turn to such mechanisms in Part III of this book.

3.4   Goal structures

Goal structures are a form of knowledge structure, held in procedural memory, which encode plans of action. These knowledge structures fulfil the same purpose in the ACT* system as the goal-related schemas fulfil in schema-based architectures (see Part I, Section 5.1 of this book for a description of how Norman uses goal-related schemas to account for slips of action).

Goal structures have a hierarchical organization: high-level goals are decomposed into a sequence of sub-goals, which in turn may be decomposed into lower level sub-goals, and so forth. For example, the high-level goal of 'quenching your thirst' can be decomposed into more specific goals such as 'making a cup of tea' or 'making some cordial'. These goals can in turn be decomposed into sub-goals corresponding to specific actions, such as 'filling the kettle' and 'pouring the cordial'. These hierarchical structures are stored as productions in procedural memory. The production rules of ACT* create and manipulate a hierarchical goal structure that represents the current plan of action. Attention is focused on a particular goal by making it a strong source of activation. However, unlike other sources, goals continue to be sources of activation until they are turned off by being explicitly modified by some production. The action of a production rule can shift the focus of attention from one goal to another. For example, when a goal is achieved it ceases to be a source of activation and the next goal in the structure is activated.

The current goal is part of the contents of working memory and as such is matched against the production rule conditions. This form of goal-directed processing is meant to simulate the conscious control we have over our behaviour. Anderson believes that the nature of such processing and the focus of attention it produces account for the serial nature of the overall flow of human cognition. Because we can only attend to one goal at a time, goal-directed cognitive processing is necessarily serial. Of course, the serial flow of cognition can be abruptly interrupted in an emergency when a new goal, generally associated with strong external stimulation, is temporarily established in working memory.

The current goal stored in working memory is a strong source of activation and, because the allocation of pattern-matching resources is determined by the relative levels of activation, there is a strong bias to match structures involving the goal. This means that the production rules which contain a goal as part of their conditions must match the current goal element to obtain an overall match. Also, because goals are such strong sources of activation, production rules which refer to a goal are more likely to match the contents of working memory, and to match more rapidly than those that do not refer to a goal.

Summary of Section 3

- Production systems are general computational mechanisms and provide the basis for a unitary theory of cognition.
- Anderson's ACT* system is one such unitary theory of cognition.
- The ACT* system comprises three memory systems: working memory holds the active temporary knowledge structures currently available to the system; declarative memory contains the system's permanent knowledge of the world; and procedural memory stores the system's production rules.
- Declarative memory stores temporal strings, spatial images and abstract propositions, in the form of a semantic network, referred to as a tangled hierarchy. The declarative network functions as a spreading activation mechanism.
- The most active nodes in the declarative network constitute the content of working memory.
- The contents of working memory are matched against the condition parts of all the stored production rules by the pattern matching mechanism. The degree of match is used to resolve conflicts between the applicable production rules.
- Hierarchically organized goal structures are used to represent plans of action, and to control the course of cognitive processing.

4   ACT* and human memory research

According to Anderson (1983), work on ACT* originated in his earlier work on a model of human memory called HAM. It is not surprising therefore that human memory research has been a major testing ground for the ACT* theory of cognition. We have seen that the types of representation used in ACT* correspond quite well to the different kinds of memory systems and their representation types postulated by experimental psychologists. We have indicated that ACT* has counterparts to working memory, long-term memory, schemas, memory for actions, memory for plans and prospective memory.

SAQ 13
List the counterparts to the following in ACT*:
1 Working memory.
2 Long-term memory.
3 Schemas.
4 Actions.
5 Plans.
6 Prospective memory.

The ACT* architecture also contains processes which correspond to the processes of encoding, retention, forgetting and retrieval in human memory.
1 *Encoding* in ACT* refers to the process through which cognitive units are turned into long-term memory traces. Whenever a cognitive unit is created in working memory it is only a temporary entity, but there is a fixed probability that it will become a permanent unit. Anderson justifies this fixed-probability assumption on the basis of experiments on memory which show that the length of presentation of an item (i.e. how long it is available for study) does not influence its probability of recall.

   Repeated presentations do, however, have an effect and this is reflected in ACT* by incrementing the strength of a unit in long-term storage whenever it appears again in the working memory.
2 *Retention and forgetting* are implemented in ACT* by an activation decay process. The probability of successful retrieval and the time taken to retrieve units from memory is a function of a unit's activation level. This kind of mechanism has quite a long history in memory research and is not a novel proposal from Anderson. The decay of a memory trace has always been the most natural way of thinking about forgetting.
3 *Retrieval* of an item in an experiment constitutes a behavioural act. In ACT*, this corresponds to a unit being matched by a production which will generate the external behavioural action of reporting

the item, perhaps verbally. Paired-associate retention of word lists, a widely used technique in memory experiments, might provide an example. If the words *book* and *student* are associated with each other at presentation time, then one might model this in ACT* through establishing a production rule:

IF the stimulus word presented is *book*
THEN say the word *student*.

Apart from these basic memory processes that are parts of the ACT* architecture itself, the model has also been used to explain experimental findings that are not built into the system. This latter kind of evidence is of course needed to check the validity of ACT* as a psychological theory — otherwise the explanations would be tautological.

Many experiments have shown that a good way of improving memory performance is to *elaborate* on the material to be remembered at the time of presentation. For example, if a subject is given a pair of items *dog–chair* as a paired associate for later recall when cued with one of these words, memory will be better if the experimental subject attempts to elaborate some coherent cognitive structure in which both words are embedded. This might be some episode in which the subject's pet dog Spot was tearing a chair, or the fact that dogs are frequently forbidden to sleep on chairs. An example of such an elaborative story has been shown earlier in network form in Figure 2.7.

Anderson argues that improved performance in experiments of this kind may be due to three different kinds of processes:
1 *Redirection of activation*: The work on elaborations may direct processing away from interfering paths of associations and towards the target path.
2 *Focusing of activation*: Activation is contributed from nodes that are not parts of the retrieval cue but which are parts of the elaborated story recalled at the time of the test.
3 *Reconstruction*: The subject reconstructs or infers what the target node must have been, using elaborations retrieved at the time of the test.

Let us now illustrate the three processes itemized above that Anderson claims are responsible for the performance advantage coming from using elaborations:
1 *The redirection of activation* towards the target is illustrated in Figure 2.7 through the presence of prior associates of *dog* that are assumed to be irrelevant to the *dog–chair* pairing in the experiment.
2 *The focusing of activation* yields more paths connecting *dog* and *chair* which help to channel activation from *dog* to *chair* instead of the other prior associates. Anderson has shown, using the spreading activation mechanism built into ACT*, that the activation arriving at *chair* and

dog will be greater than it would be if there were only a single link connecting *dog* and *chair*.

The elaborative structure in Figure 2.7 also illustrates how, when *dog* is presented as a retrieval cue, *chair* may be retrieved, even if the subject cannot directly remember it, by reproducing the elaboration at the time of the test and using the nodes in this new structure to pump more activation into it. For example, if the subject recalls that *the dog loved its master*, then *master* might be the source of additional activation for *chair* through the links in the structure. Experiments on configural cueing, in which the retrieval cue contains several elements from such a structure, have shown that there is a performance advantage.

3 *The inferential reconstruction* process predicts that manipulations that increase the use of elaborations should increase the level of both recall and intrusion errors, and Anderson reviews experiments confirming this prediction.

Anderson shows a group of thirteen production rules that could generate elaborations. The process involves creating an analogical mapping between a schema retrieved from declarative memory and the material presented. In the example in Figure 2.7, the schema is *Spot tearing the chair*, which will be mapped to the *dog–chair* pair by identifying *Spot* with *dog* and *chair* with the specific chair that Spot tore. Various other embellishments contained in the schema are also added.

The computations carried out by these thirteen production rules are summarized in Figure 2.8 in the form of a flow diagram. The productions themselves are indicated by the arrows connecting the boxes, labelled P1 to P13. The boxes are best thought of as major stages of the computation to be carried out by means of the productions. You need only gather the general contents of this computation, rather than study all the details of it. Look at each of the boxes to identity what these main stages are: embellishment, making a correspondence, etc.

Other theorists have proposed that such elaborations are produced through the use of schema-based memory systems. Anderson uses this example to show that production systems can be used to produce the same effects as schema mechanisms. This is an interesting example of *functional equivalence* between different representation systems.

SAQ 14

To check whether you understood what functional equivalence means, suppose that you have eventually managed to make that proverbial cup of tea, added the milk and now wish to stir it, but have no spoon. Name any objects that might be found on your desk that would be functionally equivalent to the spoon for this purpose.

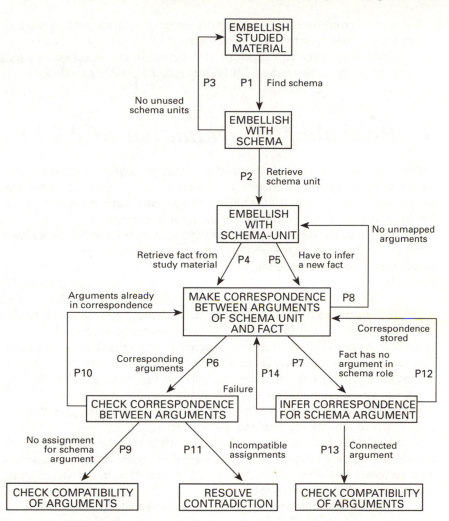

Figure 2.8   The computations involved in creating an elaborative structure (Anderson, 1983)

Summary of Section 4

- The ACT* architecture has features that correspond to a variety of memory *systems* and to the basic memory *processes* of encoding, retention and forgetting, and retrieval.
- The ACT* architecture has been used to model experimental findings on human memory.
- Anderson's account of the effects of elaboration on memory per-

formance combines the use of production system and spreading activation mechanisms in a novel way.

- Production systems can produce the same effects as schemas when appropriately programmed, illustrating functional equivalence.

5   Psychological evaluation of ACT*

While a production system architecture is in principle an abstract one, used for the purpose of implementing a computer program, it is natural for psychologists to consider whether this architecture is a good model for human cognition. Some analogies clearly emerge.

The major advantage of production systems as a basis for explaining high-level cognition is the *modular* nature of production rules. New rules can be added to procedural memory, as and when required by the model builder, with little significant effect on the rest of the system. To apply ACT* to a new piece of cognitive behaviour, the model builder needs to determine the underlying factual knowledge and add it to declarative memory, and to identify the appropriate sequence of production rules and goal structures and append them to procedural memory. The new procedural knowledge does not interfere with existing production rules. Even if the new goal structures conflict with existing ones, the system should function smoothly because the potential interference will be dealt with by the constraints built into the structure of goal-directed processing and the pattern matcher.

The working memory in a production system may be compared with the short-term working memory postulated in many cognitive theories. The activation rules can be thought of as the basic processing mechanisms underlying cognition.

Production systems are versatile, general-purpose computational devices, capable of modelling any aspect of cognition. However, not all theoreticians believe that such versatility is a virtue (Fodor, 1983). The very flexibility of production systems makes them too powerful as models of human cognition. For example, one of the production rules used by Anderson (1983) is:

IF the goal is to do a list of problems
THEN set as a sub-goal to do the first problem in the list.

Although this rule seems sensible it is somewhat arbitrary, and actually condenses and masks a history of learning and planning experiences. If there are no constraints on the creation of production rules, then where are the constraints on human cognition to be found? Of course, Anderson would argue that the cognitive system consists of more than just a collection of production rules, and that the constraints associated with human cognition are derived from the other components of the architecture, such as the constraints of processing only one goal at a time, and the conflict-resolution principles programmed into the pattern matcher.

One might also argue, as a criticism of the use of production systems in ACT*, that often the computations needed by the ACT* model could just as well be expressed in other programming languages. If you look back at Figure 2.8, for example, there is nothing in this flow-chart that dictates it must be programmed using production rules. One could just as well use other programming languages like LISP (another AI programming language, widely used in model building). This is another illustration of *functional equivalence*, this time between computer programs, but here it works against Anderson's advocacy of production systems as models of cognition. It is interesting to note that the SOAR research team now puts much less emphasis on the use of production systems and would be happy to replace it with some other functionally equivalent memory system.

The production systems approach has not concerned itself with issues relating to the capacity limitations of working memory. In the production system architecture described so far, working memory can be virtually limitless, yet all the evidence from psychological investigations suggests a limited capacity of human short-term memory. These issues must, of course, arise if production systems are regarded as a model of human cognition. For example, to simulate human problem solving, the model would have to incorporate a limit to the number of conditions which could be contained in working memory at any one time. Capacity limitations have, however, emerged in a different way in work on production systems: they are related to the bottleneck of the matching process. As was indicated in Section 3.3, this bottleneck may result from using serial rather than parallel computers for constructing models. The computation in humans may be done in a parallel fashion.

We have also described how the ACT* framework has been applied to research on human memory. It should be noted that these applications do not constitute a strong test of the *framework* as a whole, because in most cases the explanation of experimental findings only appeals to one or another aspect of the ACT* architecture in isolation. For example, the spreading activation mechanism is carrying the major part of the explanatory power in relation to memory research findings. The only instance where both spreading activation and production rules are *jointly* used is the case of elaborative processing in recall. More examples of this kind are needed.

More recently, Anderson has attempted to correct some of the shortcomings of the ACT* account of memory by concentrating on memory as an adaptive, rational process (Anderson, 1989a). In this novel framework, the memory system is regarded as an optimized solution to the information-retrieval task that the human memory system faces. He argues that the memory system uses statistics derived from past experience to predict what memories are currently relevent.

In general, ACT* provides a well-specified account of many aspects of cognition, but it must be remembered that it is only a transitory stage in working towards an integrated explanation of cognition within the production system framework. Several aspects of it have already been modified, yielding the next model, PUPS (described in Anderson, 1989b).

Summary of Section 5

- Production systems are plausible models of the long-term procedural memory system. Their main advantage is that of modularity.
- The working memory in a production system has a similar role to that of working memory in other theories.
- Production systems may be too flexible and lack constraints like those present in the human system. Moreover, production systems are functionally equivalent to other ways of programming. Anderson has used the production system to produce elaborations in memory experiments. Other programming languages could just as well have been used.
- Capacity limitations appear in a different form in production systems, as limitations resulting from the expensive nature of the matching process on serial processors. It is not clear what in ACT* corresponds to the limited capacity of human short-term memory.
- The applications of ACT* to memory research do not constitute a strong test of the theory as a whole (or of the architecture as a whole) since these applications rely mainly on the activation mechanism. An exception is the application to elaborations in recall.
- Other shortcomings of ACT* have prompted Anderson to start on a different approach, looking at memory as an adaptive, rational design for information retrieval.
- ACT* is only a transitory stage in an evolutionary succession of theories.

Further reading

ANDERSON, J. (1983) *The Architecture of Cognition*, Harvard University Press.

NEWELL, A. (1973) 'Production systems: models of control structures', in W. Chase (ed.) *Visual Information Processing*, Academic Press.

Part III
Parallel Distributed Processing and Its Application in Models of Memory

Martin Le Voi

Part III   Parallel Distributed Processing

Contents

1   *Inspirations for cognitive modelling*

Cognitive modelling is an essential part of theorizing in psychology. It consists of generating representations of knowledge, mechanisms of processing and organizational structures which are capable of processing information and producing behaviour which psychologists believe models human behaviour. There are many forms of cognitive modelling, some of which we have already seen in this book. The working memory system (Part IIA) is an example of a cognitive model which is designed to simulate or explain human behaviour in various specific tasks. Experiments which demonstrate human capabilities or failings in terms of digit span, articulatory suppression and phonemic similarity effects are simulated by means of limited capacity articulatory and phonemic slave systems and a central executive. Similarly, cognitive models expressed in terms of schemas (Part I) attempt to explain features of human memory such as selection, abstraction (or *generalization*), integration and normalization. A model of memory based on schemas would be expected to produce the same distortions of recall as humans exhibit when remembering items seen in an office (Techniques Box D, Part I). The value of cognitive models rests on how well they mimic or simulate human behaviour, and some experiments are designed to test a specific cognitive model.

Cognitive models do not appear out of thin air. They are generally born out of current scientific and technological knowledge. Before electricity was discovered, models of the brain, believe it or not, relied on systems of pumps and valves to explain behaviour! More recent models likened the brain to gigantic telephone exchanges or used flow diagram models derived from computer programming. Each of these models was *inspired* by well-understood physical systems of the day. Recently, inspiration for cognitive models has come from successes in computer programs which model artificial intelligence, and also from an improved understanding of brain microstructure, or 'neural networks'. These kinds of models are generally 'tested' by implementing them in a computer and seeing how well their behaviour could then reproduce or 'simulate' certain aspects of human behaviour.

1.1   *The rule-based approach*

Artificial intelligence attempts to create behaviour by a computer which mimics (*simulates*) the behaviour of a natural intelligence: namely ourselves. The modern approach has attempted to create this behaviour in the computer by programming it with a large collection of *rules*, and it is the sequential activation of these rules which produces behaviour more or less like that of the intended target, such as an expert medical diagnostician (an example of an expert system). Models like ACT*, based on systems of production rules, are used to develop models of how human beings learn, think and solve problems.

In these models (see Part IIB, Sections 2 and 3), large and complex collections of production rules process incoming information, adding to and subtracting from internal memory systems, and in so doing they are able to simulate human behaviour in areas of memory, language and problem solving. Part IIB describes how Anderson's ACT* model simulated human performance in learning paired associates by elaboration (Section 4), showing that such results could be produced by alternative models to those based on schema memory systems.

To achieve better and more accurate models of human performance, rule-based systems could grow more extensive sets of production rules and larger declarative memory systems, seemingly without limit. In principle, it seemed that all human behaviour could potentially be simulated by a sufficiently complicated rule-based system.

However, despite the obvious power of these approaches, some psychologists had nagging doubts as to whether this was an appropriate way to model human cognition, irrespective of whether it could successfully produce an artificial intelligence. For example, Anderson's ACT* system has a 'working memory' which is part of the model (see Figure 2.5 in Part IIB). But unlike the psychological phenomenon of working memory described in Part IIA, ACT*'s working memory is not capacity limited (see Part IIB, Section 5). So in order to simulate the human characteristics of working memory, 'the model would have to incorporate a limit' (Part IIB, p. 111). Building in limits and other features of human behaviour like this successfully produces more accurate models, but it is an essentially arbitrary process which gives no insight into the underlying reasons *why* humans have a capacity limitation in working memory in the first place.

Another good example which will figure prominently in this chapter is the modelling of learning mechanisms such as *generalization*. Generalization is a fundamental aspect of human cognition. In Part I, Section 3.3, the process of *abstraction* was described such that 'information in memory tends to undergo transformation from the specific to the *general*' (my italics). The example given was how, when trying to recall a particular visit to a restaurant, we tend to recall the general features common to many such visits, rather than the specific details of one. This is one of the ways, described in Part I, in which schemas affect memory. How these characteristics of memory and schemas are modelled lies behind the evaluation of parallel distributed processing (PDP) models compared with rule-based ones. Generalization, for example, is programmed in to the ACT* model as a way of creating more general rules from specific ones, and this has to be done because generalization is a well-known aspect of human cognition. But again, while *programming in* procedures for 'doing' generalization may successfully produce human-like behaviour, it gives no insight into how or why humans do it, seemingly effortlessly. Therefore, some psychologists consider that such rule-based systems offer essentially no insight into how knowledge is represented in the brain (Smolensky, 1988, p. 5). In the words of Hanson and Burr (1990, p. 472), 'The rule-based approach may not yet be bankrupt when it comes to learning, but cheques have bounced'.

1.2 'Neural' networks

To try to devise models which do offer insights into human behaviour, the *parallel distributed processing* (*PDP*) method spurned the capability and potential of the rule-based approach whose inspiration lay in the power of computational, but essentially *artificial*, machines (i.e. computers). The PDP approach took a much closer look at the micro-structure of the brain itself, to see if insights into the power of a natural information-processing engine such as the brain might provide a better, and hopefully more realistic, modelling system. Most psychologists are familiar with the general structure of individual neurons, with dendrites, axons and synapses, but researchers in PDP modelling were most interested in how these individual components might operate *collectively* to provide an information-processing capability.

Figure 3.1 shows a typical source of inspiration. Signals arrive on incoming axons and project on to a collection of six neurons (in this case), forming a network. If only it were possible to fathom the information-processing properties of such *neural networks*, a model of human

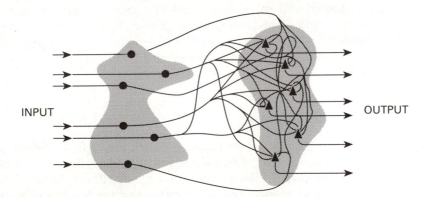

Figure 3.1   A typical 'neural network' (adapted from Anderson *et al.*, 1977)

cognition inspired by a *natural*, rather than an artificial, intelligence could be developed. When models such as these were developed, they were found to have some remarkable properties, many of which are known to be characteristics of human behaviour. For example, PDP models were found to be intrinsically capable of *generalizing* from many specific cases. This *intrinsic* generalization didn't require arbitrary specific extra add-ons to the model so that it could 'do' generalization: rather, generalization was one of the *natural* behaviours of PDP models. If you build a PDP model, as we shall see, it is automatically capable of generalization. There are other remarkable properties which we shall find are inherent in PDP models, such as schema-based learning. All these properties are known to be natural behaviour of human cognition, so psychologists were immediately attracted by a cognitive model whose *natural* properties seemed closely related to the known properties of natural intelligence. Psychologists immediately wanted to know more about the full capabilities of such a cognitive modelling system, and it is the foundations of the systematic exploration of these information-processing properties which I shall present here.

2   Local and distributed representation

The adult human brain loses hundreds of thousands of neurons every day. But despite that loss, our cognitive processes continue unaffected. We don't generally wake up unable to speak, or with large areas of vision lost, unless there is massive damage to the brain through accident or disease. The brain is robust to the loss of parts of its information-processing potential and increasing levels of damage usually produce a slowly increasing loss of performance rather than a sudden, catastrophic impairment. This slow loss of performance is called *graceful degradation*, and is one of the hallmarks of *distributed*, rather than *local* representation.

2.1   Local representation

In the schema-based models introduced in Part I, the representation of knowledge is *local*. A schema has slots, into which various items of knowledge are dropped. So the schema for a picnic (Part I, Figure 1.4) has slots for various concepts, such as the place and the food, which are related to form the schema. Each slot takes a single concept to fill it.

The contents of these slots are localized: they do not interact with the contents of each other.

Production system models are also local. Looking at the ACT* model, we can consider that the procedural memory contains all the production rules available to the ACT* cognitive system. All of these rules are individual entities, separate and distinct from each other. Rules can be added to and subtracted from the procedural memory, but addition and subtraction of new rules has no effect on the other old rules in the system, even if these new rules are combinations of old rules. It is in this sense that the rules are local, since their existence is confined to one location in procedural memory, and they have no effect on other rules unless they are activated by the execution process.

Neural models can also be local. An example of a local representation in perception comes from the 'grandmother cell hypothesis'. Work pioneered by researchers Hubel and Wiesel (1959, 1962) has shown that neurons in the cat's brain selectively respond to more and more complex visual attributes as recordings are made 'deeper' in the visual cortex. Beginning with cells in the retina responding to areas of light, subsequent layers of neurons respond to more complex patterns of light falling on the retina, progressing through so-called complex and hypercomplex cells which respond to more complex parts of the retinal image. It is as if each layer is taking the processing outputs of the previous layer and processing them to a higher level of representation. Could it be that cells would be found that respond selectively to highly specific complex stimuli, such as your own grandmother? In other words, when your grandmother comes into your field of vision, the neurons would process the information up through levels of progressively greater complexity until one neuron fires in recognition: the so-called 'grandmother cell'. This single cell would therefore selectively respond to your grandmother as a stimulus, and by extension other cells would respond to other complex stimuli, such as your father, the neighbour's cat, and so on. The perception of these objects would be said to be *localized* in the single neuron.

Although this is a clear example of a local model of perception, there are many problems with this view which meant that it never gained much ground. Apart from the fact that the discovery of neurons selectively responding to ever more integrated or abstract parts of the scene seemed to run out of steam after a certain level, and that experiments such as these could never be done on humans, the whole idea of the perception of objects being confined to the response of a single cell such as the 'grandmother cell' seemed fundamentally unsound.

Consider an alien coming to earth, who hears that the final of the Lawn Tennis Championship is being played. The alien wants to know where. 'At Wimbledon', you say. 'Where in Wimbledon?' 'On the

Centre Court.' Although you think that may suffice, the alien, ignorant of the game of tennis, continues, 'Where on the Centre Court?' 'Well, all over,' you say. 'But I want to know exactly where on the Centre Court: was it on this blade of grass or that?'

These questions are absurd because, as you know, tennis is played *all over* the tennis court, and not just on some individual blade of grass. Play is *distributed* over the whole area. In the same way, the action of perception (and memory and other human behaviour) comes about from the functioning of the whole brain, indeed perhaps the whole organism. Attempts to localize a particular perception to a single cell are simply inappropriate (e.g. Tulving, 1991).

SAQ 15
(a) If recognition of your grandmother was governed by the activity of a single cell in your brain, would you need one for every grandmother, indeed every person you know?
(b) How would the general concept 'grandmother' be represented?
(c) What would happen if that cell died?

2.2 Distributed representation

Let's look at an example of a distributed representation. Nowadays, we've all seen digital watch faces, either on our wrists or their equivalent on clocks in public places such as railway stations. Instead of using complete single digits for each number, as on a traditional clock, each number in such a display is represented by activity across seven segments (or *units*) which make it up (see Figure 3.2). Every unit is involved in the representation of each number, either by being on or off. Depending on activity in other segments, each one may form part of an edge, an angle or a closed loop. Representation of each number is *distributed* over all seven segments: no single unit selectively represents one of the numerals. In the same way, it is suggested that representation of memories in the human brain is distributed over a collection of

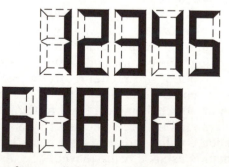

Figure 3.2 Figures from a digital watch face

individual units and their connections. These units in the brain would be the neurons and their synapses. Such a model of the way knowledge is distributed over the whole brain is sometimes known as a 'neural network'.

2.3   What are the advantages of distributed representations?

Distributed representations have a number of advantages. In the digital watch example, seven units are used to represent the ten numerals. This is an improvement over a system which needs a separate unit for each numeral. So there is some *economy* in a distributed system.

Another advantage of a distributed system is that all is not lost if there is any deterioration in the stimulus signal or loss of individual units. Suppose there is a single unit which responds to the numeral 7. If the target display is slightly distorted it may not be recognized by such a selective single unit. However, if knowledge about the numeral 7 is distributed over seven units as in Figure 3.2, even if one of these cells fails the other cells can still make sure the message gets across. This capability to continue correct operation despite the loss of parts of the information results from the fact that the original representation encoded more information than was required to maintain the representation: this is known as *redundancy* in the encoding. Figure 3.3 shows how some of the redundancy in the representation of the digital figures means that, although some information might be lost, enough is still available distributed over the seven units to allow recognition in certain circumstances of damage (but not all).

When very large numbers of units are involved, such as is the case for neurons in the brain, distributed representations are highly robust

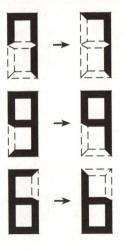

Figure 3.3   Resistance to some damage: the figures on the right are still recognizably the same as the figures on the left

to damage, which is just as well considering hundreds of thousands of brain cells die every day in the adult human. The gradual deterioration in performance (*graceful degradation*) of a distributed system, in contrast to the catastrophic failure which occurs in most conventional computers when even a single critical instruction or component is faulty, is one of its strengths. It also seems to be a characteristic of the human brain, since impairment from disease, damage, stress, ageing or shock is generally very gradual, or partial, rather than catastrophic.

Summary of Section 2

- Computational models of the brain began with models based on the rule-based approach, such as ACT*, which by and large used localized, serial computation.
- Some psychologists wanted to develop models which bore a close resemblance to the neural architecture of the brain, so they developed neural network models based on parallel distributed processing.
- Distributed models generally have redundant encoding. Information is not confined to particular locations, and performance is still possible when the network is incomplete. These models exhibit graceful degradation when damaged, which is also a characteristic of the human cognitive system.

3   *Parallel processing*

In Part I, Gillian Cohen introduced a theory of memory called schema theory. Experiments like that of Brewer and Treyens (1981) showed how these schemas are used to organize recall. In those experiments, subject were introduced to rooms containing a few cues, and they *generalized* from those cues to an organizing schema for the room, such as a kitchen schema or an office schema. Such generalization is a very important aspect of human cognition, and in this section we shall see how parallel processing models can display generalization from simple cues to general schema, using simple mechanisms of *pattern matching* and *pattern association*.

3.1   Pattern matching

As we shall see, PDP models are particularly good at *pattern matching*, especially when only the 'best fit' match is needed rather than an absolutely precise match. However, pattern matching is an essential

component of many cognitive models. Production systems like ACT*
contain a procedural memory with the rules stored individually and
separately. In order to determine which rule will fire next, the *match
process* compares the active data in *working memory* with the production rules stored in procedural memory. No rule can be left out of
the search. This process is lengthy and costly because the comparison
has to be done on an individual one-by-one basis, and is essentially a
serial one. The match process calculates the match between the *pattern*
of data in working memory, and the *pattern* of each rule's condition
part, and compares the exactness of the match, also on an individual
basis, until the best match is found (see Part IIB, Section 3.3). The
process is repeated through all the rules to find the best match, and the
rule with the best match is the next one to 'fire'. This pattern-matching
process is the most time-consuming computation performed in ACT*.

SAQ 16
How is pattern matching used in schema models of memory? (*Hint:* think of the
schema selection process.)

3.2   Simple associators

In any memory system, not just production system models, in which
the desired response or memory is retrieved by means of some cueing
process, this pattern-matching process is vital. The retrieval process
has to check the cue against all the memories stored, and produce the
most appropriate one: in other words, the response which is correctly
associated with the cue. For example, when you see a friend's face, you
have to use that cue to retrieve the correct name associated with that
face. We shall see (in Section 4) that this pattern matching and association is handled elegantly and neatly by PDP models. In these models, the match is performed against all the stored patterns in a single
step, producing direct retrieval of the associated pattern by parallel
processing. The first such PDP model we shall consider is called, conveniently, the *pattern associator*. A pattern associator is simply a device
which takes particular input patterns and associates them with the
desired output patterns. For convenience these patterns are conven-
tionally represented as number sequences (e.g. 00, or 01).

TECHNIQUES BOX K

The Pattern Associator

Figure 3.4a is an example of one of the simplest possible pattern
associators. Inputs to two input units (units Y and units Z) are processed by them to provide inputs to the output unit (only one in this

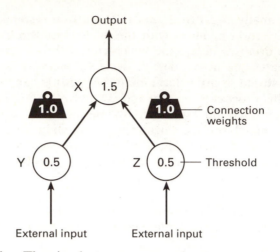

Figure 3.4a   The simplest pattern associator

case: X) which integrates them to form the output pattern. In this example, the units are *linear threshold units*. The 'threshold' description means, for each unit, if its total input when added together exceeds its threshold (which is a simple numerical value), the unit turns on (and its output is 1), otherwise it is off (and its output is 0). Only these two levels of activity are allowed. In the figure, the threshold for each unit is written inside its circle. The 'linear' description means that the total input to a unit is a simple sum over all the inputs to it. For this sum, the input values are modified or *weighted* by a simple numerical value: if the weight is 2, then the input value is modified by multiplying it by 2; if the weight is a half, then the input value is halved. A weight of 1 means the input value is unchanged (since multiplying a number by 1 results in the same value). After modifications by the weights (a process called *weighting*), the inputs of the two units are added together to get the total input. In Figure 3.4b, the output unit has two inputs, one from unit Y and one from unit Z, both weighted identically at +1, and its total input is the sum of these. The weights are written beside the connection from one unit to another. We can see this if we look at what happens if various input patterns are 'presented' to the input units Y and Z. As shown in Figure 3.4b, if the pattern presented is 1 (to Y) and 1 (to Z) (which we shall write 11), then the input activity to Y exceeds the threshold of that unit (0.5). That unit therefore turns on and presents an activity of 1 to its connection to the output unit X. The same happens to unit Z. The input activity 1 exceeds its threshold (also 0.5), so the unit turns on and presents an activity of 1 to the connection it has with the output unit X.

Output unit X has two inputs to deal with. The input activity from unit Y (1) is multiplied by its weight (also 1) giving the value of 1, and this value is *added to* (this is the meaning of the term *linear* in

the description 'linear threshold unit') the same calculation performed on the activity coming from unit Z. That calculation (activity
1 multiplied by weight 1) also gives the result 1, so adding these
values together gives a *total input* of 2. This is compared with the
output unit X's threshold (1.5), and since it is larger, the output unit
turns on and provides the output activity or response, which in this
case is therefore 1.

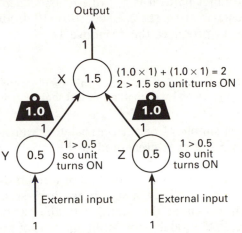

Figure 3.4b Response of associator to input 1 1

A similar calculation is illustrated in Figure 3.4c, for the input
activity pattern 01 (this means an input activity of 0 is presented to
Y, and input activity 1 is presented to Z), in which case the output
response is 0. Similar calculations for input patterns 10 and 00 also
show that the output response to these patterns is also 0.

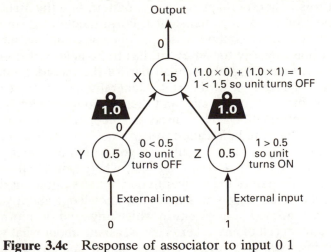

Figure 3.4c Response of associator to input 0 1

SAQ 17
Do the calculation for the input pattern 10.

Even this simple *two-layer* network model can store associations. This one is configured by its weights to store *two* associations. If the input pattern is 01, 10 or 00, these patterns are *associated with* the output 0. If, however, the input pattern is 11, this is *associated with* the output pattern 1. In memory terms, the *cues* 00, 01 or 10 produce the response 0, while the cue 11 produces the response 1.

SAQ 18
Can you think of other associations which this simple network could store, if correctly configured (such as by changing the thresholds, or weights)?

So even this most simple of pattern associators can store two associations, such that various cues presented at the input give rise to various responses at the output. What is interesting is how such networks behave when they have many units with lots of weights attached. Eysenck and Keane (1990, p. 241) have a simple worked example of a pattern associator which associates the 'sight' with the 'scent' of a rose, and which shows this PDP model associating patterns of greater complexity than the ones discussed here so far. However, in Section 3.3 we shall look at a more complex example used to demonstrate the operation of schemas in memory. First we need to understand how to extend the analysis of a pattern associator to a simple 'auto-associator'.

Pattern associators are useful when we want to form an association between one complete pattern and another (e.g. to link one, perhaps visual, pattern to another, perhaps olfactory, pattern like the association of the 'smell' of a rose with its 'sight'). For a model of memory, however, one of the most common uses is when a complete set of information, such as memory for an event, has to be held in memory, and then later retrieved using just a small part of the recorded information as a *cue* for recall of all the rest. Generally, any part of the information may form part of the cue, and there is no way of knowing which part of the information will be used as a cue, or which part of the information will need to be recalled. As an example, suppose I ask you questions about your home. I could ask you to tell me what you have in your living room, or I could ask you where you keep your books. Whether or not part of the answer to one of these questions was the cue used in the other, the point is that your knowledge about your home needs to be encoded in a system in which any kind of information can be used for recall of any other. That is, asking about what you keep in your living room may recall books as part of the answer, and one of the answers to asking where you keep books may be your living room. The PDP model most suited for this capability is the *auto-associator*.

TECHNIQUES BOX L

The Auto-associator

The pattern associator in Figure 3.4 can be redrawn as an auto-associator network as in Figure 3.5. You can see that every unit provides an input on to every other unit in the network, in this case with only one layer of units. The network projects its own output activity on to *itself* (hence the prefix 'auto-' (Greek for 'self') in 'auto-associator'). Unit X transmits its output on to Y and Z and itself, unit Y sends its output to X and Z and itself, and unit Z sends it output to X and Y and itself. (Sometimes, the connection of a neuron on to itself is omitted.)

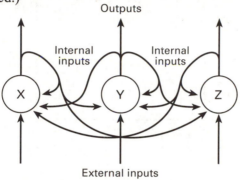

Figure 3.5   An auto-associative network

Otherwise the network is much the same as the pattern associator, except there is now no distinction between input and output units. Instead of associating input patterns (00, 01 and 10 with 0) and (11 with 1), it simply stores the patterns 000, 010, 100 and 111, with no distinction between input and output units. We are interested in how the network will *complete* a pattern presented to it with some of the information missing. This is like my asking you what you keep in your living room: you have to recall the missing information. In this case, we could use cues such as 00x or 11x, which correspond to the cues 00 and 11 used in the pattern associator. The 'x' means the information is unspecified (not part of the cue) and we want to see if the network will complete the patterns appropriately, producing complete patterns 000 and 111. This would be like recalling that you have books in your living room. What makes this different from the pattern associator is that we can cue with other patterns such as x11. Again, we are interested in completion of the pattern at x. This would be like asking you where you keep your books. A response can be retrieved to any part of the input pattern used as a cue: this is what makes the auto-associator different from the pattern associator.

The network can equally well respond to cues applied to any of the units and it will naturally provide a response over the unspecified units, as a memory system requires (see beginning of Section 3.2). Human memory is generally able to respond to cues made up from any part of a stimulus or event, so the network at least superficially seems to behave like natural memory.

We shall look at the behaviour of a large auto-associator designed to operate as a schema memory system. However, in order to understand the behaviour of a large auto-associative network, we need

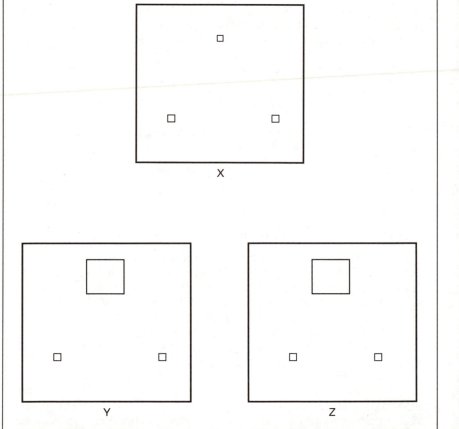

Figure 3.6   A Hinton diagram for a three-unit pattern associator. Inside each very large square, one for each of the units, X, Y and Z, there are three small squares. These small squares represent the connection weight from that unit on to each of the three units in the network: each unit has a connection to the other two units and also to itself (see Figure 3.7)

to find a simple summary which depicts all of the connections between the units. *Hinton diagrams* (Hinton and Sejnowski, 1986) use the method shown in Figure 3.6, which is explained in Figure 3.7. Every unit in the network is represented by a very large square, emphasized in the figures by a thicker border. These figures represent the connections of the three-unit auto-associator in Figure 3.5. So the three very large squares represent the three units X, Y and Z, and are labelled as such.

These three very large squares are arranged in a triangle in the figure. Now, looking again at Figure 3.5, we can see that each unit in

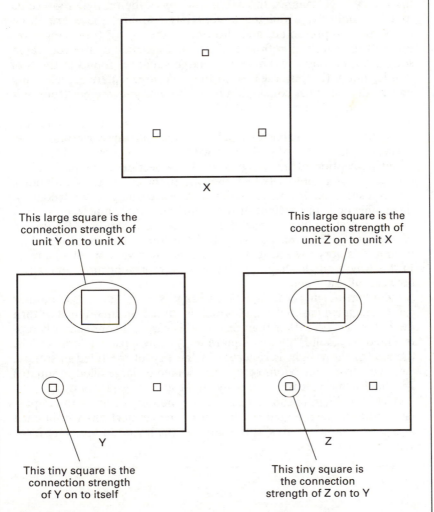

Figure 3.7   Some of the connections from the individual units are labelled to indicate what they represent

129

the network sends information to or *connects to* every other unit in the network (including itself). When each unit connects to another unit, it does so with a certain *weight* or *connection strength*, just as in the pattern associator example.

Inside each very large square in Figures 3.6 and 3.7 is a representation of the weight or connection strength from that unit on to all the others. As there are three units, then the very large square representing each unit will 'contain' three connection strengths, one for each connection of that unit on to all the others (including itself). These three connection strengths are arranged in a triangle in the same way as the three very large squares are. This means that, of the three very large squares, the one at the *top* of the triangle represents unit X. Similarly, within each very large square, there are three connections represented, and the one at the *top* of the triangle represents the connection *from* that unit (as specified by the very large square) *on to* that unit whose very large square is found at the top, that is, unit X (in this case). So in the very large square representing unit Z, the top-most connection is the *connection strength* from unit Z on to unit X (since it is unit X's very large square which is found at the top of the Hinton diagram). In Figure 3.7, four of the connection strengths have been explicitly labelled to illustrate this correspondence.

Rather than clutter the diagram with lots of numbers, and to allow easier perception of the weights, each connection strength is represented, not as a number (which they are in the computer simulation), but as a small square which varies in size according to the weight of the connection. The weight of the connection from unit Z on to unit X is very high, so it is a much larger square □. Similarly for unit Y on to unit X. However, the weight of the connection from unit Y on to unit Z is very low, so it is represented by a very small square ▫. In this way, a single shape can be used to represent the connections between all the units.

Note that weights or connection strengths from one unit to another can be negative (so that a unit which is turned on then tends to turn the other unit off rather than on). In this case the connection is represented by a solid, filled-in square ■. As with positive connections, the size of the weight is reflected in the size of the filled-in square: large negative connections being represented by large filled-in squares ■, small negative connections by small filled-in squares ■.

A Hinton diagram can be used for any number of units: the important thing to grasp is that the layout of the connections within each of the 'very large squares' is the same as the layout of the 'very large squares' themselves.

130

SAQ 19
In Figure 3.6, identify the connection *from* Unit Y *on to* unit Z.

You may have noticed that this method of indicating the weights of connections between units provides no representation for the *threshold* of each unit. A representation of the threshold could easily be added to the square for each unit. However, many PDP models, including the ones I will now describe, do not use threshold-based units. Instead, the output of each unit is calculated from the weighted sum of the inputs, rather than being either simply on or off (i.e. the output is *graded* rather than all-or-none).* The output of the associators we looked at previously had *all-or-none responses*: their output was either 0 or 1 or a pattern of 0 and 1s. Graded output can give any output value, although many models only allow values between −1 and +1 (e.g. 0.5, −0.2). The output firing rate of many neurons in the brain seems to be graded, and in Part I human memory appeared to show graded output, at least insofar as subjects could give confidence ratings to their answers to general knowledge questions (Part I, Techniques Box B), so this is perhaps a more plausible model.

SAQ 20
If the pattern associator in Figure 3.4 had a graded output (i.e. not controlled by a threshold) what would its output be to the input patterns 01 and 11? (Note that, as none of the units in the network uses a threshold, the output of any unit would be a simple weighted sum of its inputs, without any comparison with a threshold.)

3.3   An example of a PDP model of schema organization in memory

In Part I, the experiment by Brewer and Treyens (1981) (Techniques Box D) showed how schemas play a part in organizing our perception and recall of rooms, such as an office. They showed that we all have a good idea as to what the typical room or office looks like, and the kind of furniture and objects to expect in each type of room, and that these 'schemas' influence our ability to recall items in a room. Rumelhart, Smolensky, McClelland and Hinton (1986) devised a PDP model to illustrate how the phenomenon of the schema-based organization of knowledge *emerges* from a network of units. Their network was a simple auto-associator as in Figure 3.5, expanded to 40 units (rather than 3).

---

* The output is often altered with a simple mathematical function rather than being taken 'as is'. This is usually done as a matter of computational convenience as it makes the model easier to handle, so this technicality will not be pursued here.

131

TECHNIQUES BOX M

Schema Organization in Memory

Rumelhart *et al.* (1986) chose a set of 40 *descriptors* of rooms, which included items of furniture (sofa, oven, etc.) which might be found in them, and some attributes (such as size, or presence of windows). They asked two people to imagine a *particular* real office, and then go through the list of 40 descriptors saying if each one applied to that office. Then this was repeated with each person imagining a particular real kitchen, living room, bathroom and bedroom. This was done for 8 different real examples of each of the rooms by both people, giving 16 examples for each of the 5 room types, a grand total of 80 different room descriptions. This method wasn't intended to be an experiment of any sort. Rather, it was a rough-and-ready way to get 80 different room descriptions, to see if the items common to the different descriptions of each type of room would be reflected in the performance of an associative network, based on presenting those items to the net as input cues.

These descriptions were then condensed and stored as a series of

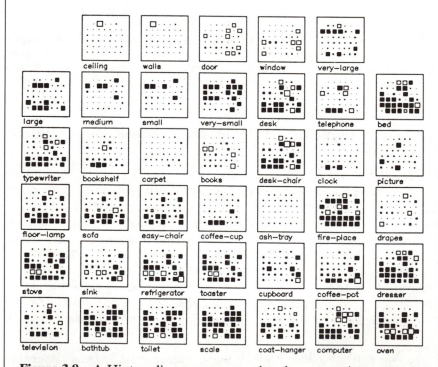

Figure 3.8   A Hinton diagram representing the connection strengths between unit descriptors (Rumelhart, Smolensky, McClelland and Hinton, 1986, p. 24)

132

weights representing the probability that every possible pairing of descriptors (such as sofa, oven) co-existed in those 80 room descriptions. The weights are represented in a Hinton diagram (see Figure 3.8). There are 40 units, corresponding to each of the 40 descriptors. Each unit connects to all of the others, and the 40 very large squares are laid out in five rows of seven and one row of five at the top. Each of these very large squares is labelled with the unit or descriptor it represents. Again each unit sends a connection to every other one, so inside each very large square are depicted 40 connection strengths. As in Figures 3.6 and 3.7, these are arranged in the same way as the very large squares: five rows of seven with a row of five on top. For example, for any particular unit, you can see the depiction of the connection *from* that unit on to the 'television' unit by looking at the small square at the bottom left inside the very large square representing that unit. This reflects the fact that the 'television' unit's representation as a very large square is situated at the bottom left in the whole diagram. Figure 3.9 explicitly labels a few of the connections. Again, strong positive connections are depicted by large open squares, strong negative connections are depicted by large filled-in squares. Weak connections are depicted by small squares.

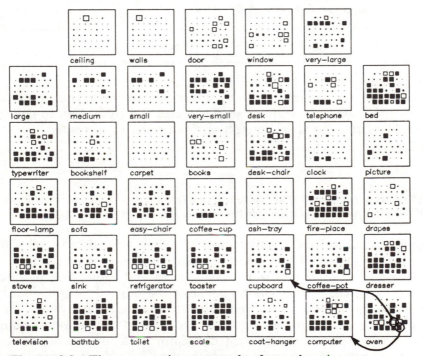

Figure 3.9 The connection strengths from descriptor oven to computer, and from oven to cupboard, are indicated (based on Rumelhart, Smolensky, McClelland and Hinton, 1986, p. 24)

In this case, strong positive connections result when two descriptors occur together more often than not in the 80 room descriptions collected by Rumelhart *et al.* For example, the descriptors oven and coffee-pot generally occurred together in the room descriptions, therefore the connection from oven to coffee-pot is a large open square (see Figure 3.9). When the presence of one descriptor generally coincides with the *absence* of the other, the result is a strong *negative* connection. Presence of a computer generally coincides with the absence of a toilet in a room, so the connection from computer to toilet is strongly negative (see Figure 3.9 again).

Looking at the 'oven' descriptor in the bottom right-hand square of Figure 3.9, we can see from the connection weights in its bottom row that it has a strongly negative relationship with bathtub, toilet, scale, coat-hanger and computer. However, it has strong positive connections with the descriptors sink, refrigerator, cupboard and coffee-pot on the next row up. Ignoring the connection of a descriptor with itself (which this particular model forces to zero), there are 1,560 connections. In this model the connection between descriptors was set the same in each direction. In other words, the connection between coffee-pot and oven was the same as the connection between oven and coffee-pot. So in all there were 780 different connection strengths in the network of 40 units.

Activity
Check that the connection strength from coffee-pot to oven uses the same kind and size of square as the connection from oven to coffee-pot. Similarly, check the connection from toilet to computer.

SAQ 21
Where is the connection from the ceiling descriptor to the walls descriptor found? What is its value? Is ceiling strongly connected to any other descriptor?

So far, this network is simply a representation of the data supplied by the human subjects. However, now we can see how such a network will respond when presented with a cue. As we said before, for an auto-associator a cue can be any fragment of the original information. In this case, the cue was the 'presentation' (turning on) of two descriptors. One of the descriptors presented to the network was always ceiling: this was paired with a different descriptor each time to create five different cues. The descriptors which were individually paired with ceiling were: oven, desk, bathtub, sofa and bed (the cue is highlighted in the results shown in Figures 3.10a to 3.10e). The simulation runs by presenting the cue, then recording the response of each unit in the network as it responds to the activity, according to the connection weights in Figure 3.8. Then that recorded pattern is presented as an input to the network: the output is said to be *fed back* to the input. The response of the network to that activity is recorded and *fed back* again to the input: this was repeated 400 times. In Figures 3.10a to 3.10e, the activity in the network units is presented after every 20 repetitions: the size of the square represents the degree of activity in the unit. The rightmost square is the final state of activity. In a system like this with large amounts of feedback, the activity in each unit could increase indefinitely unless *constrained*. In this model, activity in each unit is prevented from exceeding a predefined maximum (constrained) so the model is an example of a *constraint satisfaction network*.

For each cue, Figures 3.10a to 3.10e show how activity in the various units (the network's *response*) rises as the activity is fed back on itself, until activity ends up with a *pattern* of some units activated more or less at maximum, with others turned off. In Figure 3.10a, units ceiling and oven are turned on to form the cue. As the activity in the network is fed back repeatedly to itself, other units become active, beginning with refrigerator, sink and walls. Other units become active later in the sequence of repeated feedback: the last to do so is the clock unit. The final pattern of active units is found in the rightmost column. If we look

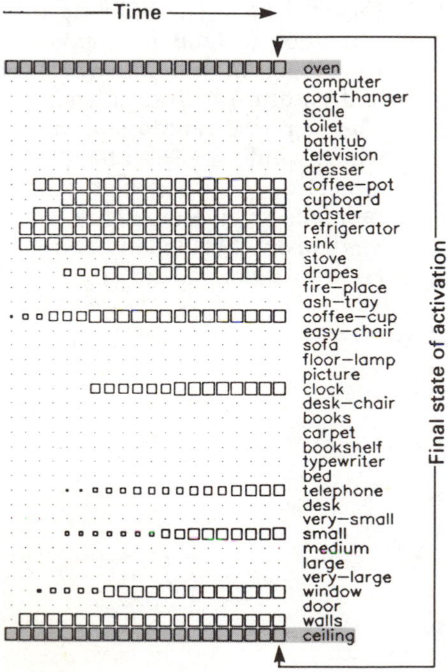

Figure 3.10a The build up of activation of units in response to turning on two units (ceiling and oven) to form a cue. The response represents activity which would apply to the typical or schematic kitchen (adapted from Rumelhart, Smolensky, McClelland and Hinton, 1986, pp. 26–7)

135

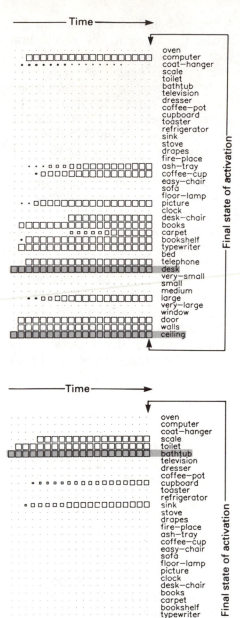

Figure 3.10b The build up of activation of units in response to turning on two units (ceiling and desk) to form a cue. The response represents activity which would apply to the typical or schematic office (adapted from Rumelhart, Smolensky, McClelland and Hinton, 1986, pp. 26–7)

Figure 3.10c The build up of activation of units in response to turning on two units (ceiling and bathtub) to form a cue. The response represents activity which would apply to the typical or schematic bathroom (adapted from Rumelhart, Smolensky, McClelland and Hinton, 1986, pp. 26–7)

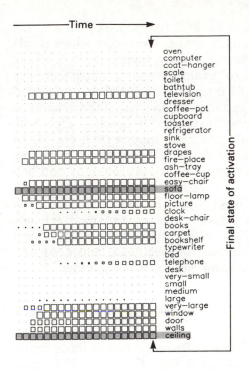

Figure 3.10d   The build up of activation of units in response to turning on two units (ceiling and sofa) to form a cue. The response represents activity which would apply to the typical or schematic living room (adapted from Rumelhart, Smolensky, McClelland and Hinton, 1986, pp. 26–7)

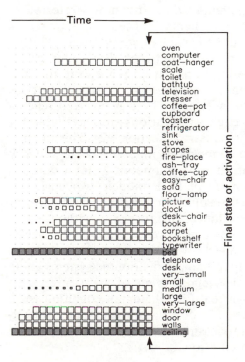

Figure 3.10e   The build up of activation of units in response to turning on two units (ceiling and bed) to form a cue. The response represents activity which would apply to the typical or schematic bedroom (adapted from Rumelhart, Smolensky, McClelland and Hinton, 1986, pp. 26–7)

137

at the results from the five cues (Figures 3.10a to 3.10e) we see that these five responses represent activity in the descriptors which would apply to the five room schemas: kitchen, office, bathroom, living room and bedroom. The first response, for example, was to ceiling and oven as a cue (Figure 3.10a), and the final result (in the rightmost column) was the activity (represented by large squares) in some of the descriptors (in this case oven, coffee-pot, cupboard, toaster, fridge, sink, etc). Note that all these descriptors become active even though oven itself (part of the original *cue*) is only strongly connected to four of them (see Figure 3.8). These items are the things you would generally find in a kitchen: they form a description of a *typical* (or schematic) kitchen.

Similarly, the other four responses (Figures 3.10b to 3.10e) are other typical rooms. None of these final responses corresponds exactly to any of the original 80 room descriptions. Also, although there are 2^{40} final possible states of this network after extensive feedback, only these five, the five 'stored schemas', emerge from cueing in this manner.

SAQ 22
What units were turned on in the final state of the network as a response to *bathtub* and *ceiling* as a cue (Figure 3.10c)?

What does this pattern of results show? The response of the network to these cues, producing the five room schemas, shows that PDP models are capable of *spontaneous generalization*. Just now I referred to the responses as being the five 'stored schemas'. I used quotation marks because these five schemas were not themselves stored at all. All that the network stored were the correlations between descriptors calculated from 80 *individual* room descriptions. At no point were the central tendencies or schema responses concealed in these descriptions explicitly derived or stored in the network. There is no fixed schema for a 'living room' or 'kitchen', each with various slots available for filling by various 'default values' (see Part I, Section 3.2). The schema-like properties *emerged* from the connections inherent in the network as it was interrogated by various cues. Spontaneous generalization is an example of an *emergent property* of PDP models. An emergent property of a model is one which results from the natural behaviour of the model under normal circumstances of processing without being explicitly built-in to the model. We have already described graceful degradation, which is another property which emerges from a representation scheme based on a highly redundant distributed system. These *emergent properties* of PDP models make them of great interest to psychologists, because well-known features of human cognition, such as schema-like representations, seem to be a natural and indeed inevitable result of an information-processing system based on parallel distributed processing and representation.

138

In the case of human cognition, the Brewer and Treyens (1981) experiment (see Part I, Section 4.1) shows that perceiving a few cues about a room context causes humans to spontaneously generalize from those cues to generate schema-like encodings of the stimuli: often 'recalling' items in a scene which were not there (such as a telephone in an office). The ability of PDP models to spontaneously generalize in much the same way is one possible explanation of why humans appear to use schemas extensively for organizing memory.

Summary of Section 3

- *Pattern matching* is a fundamental process in nearly all computational models of human cognition.
- The *pattern associator*, a simple two-layer PDP model, is well suited to doing pattern matching and generating associations in parallel between different input and output patterns.
- The one-layer *auto-associator* also performs pattern matching and storage, and is appropriate where there is no obvious definition of the input and output parts of the pattern: any part of a stored pattern may be used as a cue for retrieval of the rest.

4   *Learning*

Rumelhart *et al.*'s model did not learn. It was pre-programmed with the connections between individual units calculated directly from the 80 individual descriptions of different rooms. How much more impressive the results would be if the model had learned all by itself, by presenting the descriptions of 80 real rooms one at a time to the network, allowing it to learn and store each individual description as well as deriving the generalization of the schema. Also, human memory has another important feature. If it is presented with a partial cue, such as a picture of a face or the scent of a rose, it will recall other information to complete the cue, such as the name of the owner of the face or the appearance of a rose. The memory system has been cued with part of the *content* of the memory trace in order to produce recall. This is known as *content addressability*. When you see a friend, just the image of the face (part of the memory's content) is usually sufficient for recall of the name or other information about that person. However, alternative computational models, based on computer analogies (such as procedural models), find it difficult (though not impossible) to model content addressability, since the computer naturally addresses memory by *location*, not content: information is looked up in a computer by knowing *where* it is stored. The same is true of finding books in a library: to find one you need to know where it is stored, and finding it will require some search path according to the library's storage scheme. Content addressability, therefore, is such a central feature of human memory that any cognitive model of memory must adequately reproduce it.

Consider a child learning which animals he or she sees are called dogs, and which ones cats. The child is attempting to create the correct representation in semantic memory which identifies dogs as dogs and cats as cats. What the child actually sees is numerous individual dogs and cats (these are known as *exemplars*) which are often correctly described by a nearby adult. From these exemplars the child has to build a 'picture' progressively in semantic memory of the general characteristics of dogs as opposed to cats, or indeed any other animal or thing. This learning process is something that PDP models are particularly well suited to. We shall now look at how PDP models can learn or 'memorize' inputs and respond to cues. This is achieved by altering the weights or connection strengths in the model so that the network responds correctly to cues. Techniques Box N goes into the learning process in some detail: the details themselves are not important, as long as you understand the principle by which the weights are altered in order to allow the network to learn.

4.1   Learning by error propagation

In PDP models, learning by *error propagation* means that the network compares its output with a target output, and any difference or error is 'propagated back' to the input weights which are altered in a way that reduces the error.

TECHNIQUES BOX N

Learning by Error Propagation

It is easiest to consider the case of a three-unit auto-associator (Figure 3.5). We are going to present the input pattern (3, 1, 2) across the three units, and show how it can learn this pattern over successive presentations by using a simple rule for adjusting the connections between the units.

Following Rumelhart *et al.* above, we do not allow a unit to connect to itself, so each one makes a connection to the other two, making six connections in all. Each unit therefore *receives* two inputs, one from each of the other two units. The activity or output of a unit is determined by the activity it receives from these inputs, each one modified by a unique numerical weight.

Each learning sequence progresses as follows. The activity pattern (3, 1, 2) is impressed on the three units: Unit X has activity 3, Y activity 1, and Z activity 2. These activities spread or *propagate* along the connections to form the inputs to the other units. Each unit then adds together the inputs it receives from all the other units and produces a new activity level, which constitutes its new output*. This output activity is compared with the starting input activity pattern, and the difference (or *error*) is used to alter the connection strengths (weights) in a direction which, the next time the pattern is presented to the network, will produce an output activity much more like the input activity pattern (3, 1, 2).

Tables 3.1 and 3.2 on page 143 show how all this works. To begin with, all weights are 0. Table 3.1 shows how the activity propagates around the network. The external input pattern presented to each unit is shown in column 2.

For each unit, the activity received from the other two units is combined according to the current weights (column 5) to produce an output activity. The aim in learning is to find a set of weights which, when used to combine activity from the other units, produces an output activity pattern which is identical to the external input activity pattern. That is, the aim is to get the newly calculated output activity in column 7 to agree completely with the external input (column 2). Since the output is generally not the same as the external input, the difference (*error*) is used to calculate a new set of weights (in the last column) which should produce better agreement between the calculated output activity and the external input. Eventually, the set of weights should get close to (*converge on*) the ideal set of weights which would reproduce the external input pattern exactly.

To see how this works, it is easier to look at the calculations in Table 3.2, rather than Table 3.1, which has many zeros in it which may confuse things somewhat. Looking at Table 3.2, we can trace the modification of connection weights that result from the second presentation of the pattern. The initial values of the weights, calculated from the first presentation of the pattern (Table 3.1), is in column 5. For each unit, the inputs from the other two units (column 4) is multiplied by the appropriate weight (column 5) and added together to form the total input (column 6).

This total input is used to calculate the output of each unit. In this case, to keep it simple, the output is set the same as the input. This new output is not the same as the target input (column 2), so the weights must be changed to get the network to remember the input pattern better. Each unit's output is compared with the unit's external input (column 2), and the difference is used to calculate the change in weight. This calculation (column 9) multiplies the differ-

---

* The input calculation usually also includes the external input, which is added to the total input. For clarity, and for the purpose of illustration, this step has been omitted.

ence between output and external input (column 8) by the input from the other units (column 4) and a *learning parameter*, which is set at 0.1 in all these tables. The learning parameter is used to control how fast the network learns: so different learning rates can be modelled. The learning parameter can be between 0 and 1: larger parameters mean that the network can learn faster (i.e. from fewer presentations), but instability may result from learning parameters which are too high. When this happens, the weights oscillate between values and do not settle down on the ideal set of weights which correctly reproduce the external input. Finally, the change in weight (column 9) is added to the current weight (column 5) to give the new weight (column 10), which is used in the next presentation of an input pattern.

So in Table 3.2, unit X received an external input of 3. The internal inputs from Y and Z are 1 and 2. Each of these is multiplied by the weight for that connection (1×0.3, 2×0.6), and the two numbers added together to give the total input (1.5). Setting the output to 1.5, this is compared with the target input (3) and the difference (1.5) is used to calculate new weights. The difference is multiplied by the internal input, so the calculation for the connection from Y multiplies 1.5 by 1 and by the learning parameter (0.1). The result (0.15) is added to the current weight (0.3) to give the new weight (0.45). This is repeated down the table for each connection. The new weights then form the current weights for the third presentation, and so on.

Can this simple alteration in weights really result in a network which 'remembers' the external input? The output activity in the second presentation was getting nearer to (*converging on*) the external input pattern (3, 1, 2). The pattern was (1.5, 1.3, 2.0). And the new weights calculated from that presentation would produce an output activity even closer (it would be (2.25, 0.91, 2)). Eventually, the new weights converge on a set of weights which reproduce external input precisely.

It is important to note that this learning has taken place on the basis of purely local operations. That is, the alteration of a weight in any part of the network is due to a comparison between the actual output and desired output at that precise point of the network; no information about how well the pattern fits the target anywhere else in the network is either used or required. The fact that PDP networks can learn from such purely local operations is also a major desirable feature of a model which purports to mimic operations in the brain. In the brain, it may be surmised that neurons can only alter their connections according to the activity in adjacent neurons with which they are in communication. It seems unlikely that communication between neurons could be *directly* modified by activity elsewhere in the brain, so the brain probably learns by means of purely local operations too.

Table 3.1 Learning from first presentation of the target stimulus

Unit (1)	External input (2)	Input along connection			Input calculation			Weight change calculation	
		from unit (3)	input activity (4)	current weight (5)	Total input from connections (6)	Output activity (7)	Error (External input – Output) (8)	Change in weight (0.1 is learning parameter) (9)	New weight (Current weight + Change in weight) (10)
X	3	Y	1	0	$(1 \times 0) + (2 \times 0) = 0$	0	$3 - 0 = 3$	$3 \times 1 \times 0.1 = 0.3$	$0 + 0.3 = 0.3$
		Z	2	0				$3 \times 2 \times 0.1 = 0.6$	$0 + 0.6 = 0.6$
Y	1	X	3	0	$(3 \times 0) + (2 \times 0) = 0$	0	$1 - 0 = 1$	$1 \times 3 \times 0.1 = 0.3$	$0 + 0.3 = 0.3$
		Z	2	0				$1 \times 2 \times 0.1 = 0.2$	$0 + 0.2 = 0.2$
Z	2	X	3	0	$(3 \times 0) + (1 \times 0) = 0$	0	$2 - 0 = 2$	$2 \times 3 \times 0.1 = 0.6$	$0 + 0.6 = 0.6$
		Y	1	0				$2 \times 1 \times 0.1 = 0.2$	$0 + 0.2 = 0.2$

Table 3.2 Learning from second presentation of the target stimulus

Unit (1)	External input (2)	Input along connection			Input calculation			Weight change calculation	
		from unit (3)	input activity (4)	current weight (5)	Total input from connections (6)	Output activity (7)	Error (External input – Output) (8)	Change in weight (0.1 is learning parameter) (9)	New weight (Current weight + Change in weight) (10)
X	3	Y	1	0.3	$(1 \times 0.3) + (2 \times 0.6) = 1.5$	1.5	$3 - 1.5 = 1.5$	$1.5 \times 1 \times 0.1 = 0.15$	$0.3 + 0.15 = 0.45$
		Z	2	0.6				$1.5 \times 2 \times 0.1 = 0.3$	$0.6 + 0.3 = 0.9$
Y	1	X	3	0.3	$(3 \times 0.3) + (2 \times 0.2) = 1.3$	1.3	$1 - 1.3 = -0.3$	$-0.3 \times 3 \times 0.1 = -0.09$	$0.3 - 0.09 = 0.21$
		Z	2	0.2				$-0.3 \times 2 \times 0.1 = -0.06$	$0.2 - 0.06 = 0.14$
Z	2	X	3	0.6	$(3 \times 0.6) + (1 \times 0.2) = 2.0$	2.0	$2 - 2.0 = 0$	$0 \times 3 \times 0.1 = 0$	$0.6 + 0 = 0.6$
		Y	1	0.2				$0 \times 1 \times 0.1 = 0$	$0.2 + 0 = 0.2$

SAQ 23
If you're still not convinced that this convergence is happening, calculate the set of weights from the third presentation of the target using a table like that in Table 3.2. It may help you to know that the solution on which the weights are converging is: (0.6, 1.2, 0.2308, 0.1538, 0.6, 0.2). Perhaps you'd like to check that these weights will recreate the external input pattern correctly. It's also clear even from Table 3.2 that the weights in the model are slowly converging on these final solution weights (look especially at the new weights calculated in the last column).

The important point to grasp in all this is that, after each stimulus presentation, the network learns by gradually changing the connection weights in the appropriate direction. Eventually, the connection weights are such that the pattern is learned completely, and presenting the pattern or part of it produces error-free recall. The illustration of these calculations aims to demonstrate to you that a simple learning mechanism can be successful at deriving connection weights which can exactly reproduce the patterns presented at the input.

4.2   Emergent properties of associative networks

Even with a simple three-unit network we can illustrate some properties of these associative networks. The first is *content addressability*. If we interrogate the network with a cue consisting of only part of the input pattern, such as (3, 1, ?) we can see if it responds with the missing part. The result is indeed that the network responds with (X, X, 2), completing the pattern. The network recalls the missing fragment of the input pattern using only the cue to start its activity. This cue comes from part of the *contents* of the original pattern and is used to *address* the network for recall of a particular pattern; hence the term *content addressability*. In Section 3.3, the network was cued with parts of the original pattern (some contents) to recall the schema patterns. This is another important *emergent property* of PDP models. It has long been known that an important feature of human memory is its ability to respond to partial cues by recall of whole memories (patterns). In rule-based computer models, content addressability has to be 'programmed in', but for auto-associators based on PDP models it is a natural response of the network to partial cues. The extent to which various properties of human memory are naturally found in PDP models, rather than having to be explicitly programmed in to a computer model, is behind much of the debate as to the worth of PDP models as opposed to rule-based models of human cognition (see Section 6 and Overview).

The second property is that we didn't have to restrict ourselves to presenting one input pattern to learn. We could have used more. Table 3.3 shows the result of presenting a different pattern (0, 2, 1) to the network after the first presentation of the original pattern (3, 1, 2). The

Table 3.3 Learning from presentation of a different stimulus, after the first presentation of the old stimulus

Unit (1)	External input (2)	from unit (3)	input activity (4)	current weight (5)	Total input from connections (6)	Output activity (7)	Error (External input – Output) (8)	Change in weight (0.1 is learning parameter) (9)	New weight (Current weight + Change in weight) (10)
					Input calculation			Weight change calculation	
					Input along connection				
X	0	Y	2	0.3	$(2 \times 0.3) + (1 \times 0.6) = 1.2$	1.2	$0 - 1.2 = -1.2$	$-1.2 \times 2 \times 0.1 = -0.24$	$0.3 + -0.24 = 0.06$
		Z	1	0.6				$-1.2 \times 1 \times 0.1 = -0.12$	$0.6 + -0.12 = 0.48$
Y	2	X	0	0.3	$(0 \times 0.3) + (1 \times 0.2) = 0.2$	0.2	$2 - 0.2 = 1.8$	$1.8 \times 0 \times 0.1 = 0$	$0.3 + 0 = 0.3$
		Z	1	0.2				$1.8 \times 1 \times 0.1 = 0.18$	$0.2 + 0.18 = 0.38$
Z	1	X	0	0.6	$(0 \times 0.6) + (2 \times 0.2) = 0.4$	0.4	$1 - 0.4 = 0.6$	$0.8 \times 0 \times 0.1 = 0$	$0.6 + 0 = 0.6$
		Y	2	0.2				$0.6 \times 2 \times 0.1 = 0.12$	$0.2 + 0.12 = 0.32$

145

Table 3.4 Final response of trained net to the alternate presentation of two training stimuli. The connection weights are in bold: note that the same connection weights are used to store two different patterns

Response to first target:

Unit (1)	External input (2)	from unit (3)	input activity (4)	current weight (5)	Total input from connections (6)	Output activity (7)
			Input along connection		**Input calculation**	
X	0	Y	2	**-1**	$(2 \times -1) + (1 \times 2) = 0$	0
		Z	1	**2**		
Y	2	X	0	**-1**	$(0 \times -1) + (1 \times 2) = 2$	2
		Z	1	**2**		
Z	1	X	0	**0.5**	$(0 \times 0.5) + (2 \times 0.5) = 1$	1
		Y	2	**0.5**		

Response to second target:

Unit (1)	External input (2)	from unit (3)	input activity (4)	current weight (5)	Total input from connections (6)	Output activity (7)
			Input along connection		**Input calculation**	
X	3	Y	1	**-1**	$(1 \times -1) + (2 \times 2) = 3$	3
		Z	2	**2**		
Y	1	X	3	**-1**	$(3 \times -1) + (2 \times 2) = 1$	1
		Z	2	**2**		
Z	2	X	3	**0.5**	$(3 \times 0.5) + (1 \times 0.5) = 2$	2
		Y	1	**0.5**		

rule for calculating the change in weights remains exactly the same, but of course the new pattern changes the weights in different ways, as Table 3.3 shows (compare the new weights with those in Table 3.2). However, if we go on alternately presenting the two patterns, eventually the weights *converge* on a set which successfully stores *both* patterns perfectly. Table 3.4 shows the final set of weights which have this property. Note how the weights required to store *two* input patterns differ from the weights learned from *one* input pattern alone (listed in SAQ 23 above).

It sometimes seems odd that one set of weights, each of which is involved in the storage of both traces, can store more than one pattern. It does work though. Any system where the pattern encoding is distributed over many units can do this. An example is magnetic tape recording. Some of you may know from using open-reel tape recorders that you can make a second recording 'over the top' of an old recording, provided the erasing of the tape is disabled (this capability used to be called 'sound-on-sound'). The tape then holds a recording of two, quite different, sound images. In this case the recording is *distributed* over millions of tiny magnetic particles, all of which contribute to the recording of each sound image, as a result of changing their magnetic properties ('weights') as each signal is recorded on them. This capability of magnetic tape to record multiple images is exploited by modern 'hi-fi' video cassette recorders, in which the sound image is first recorded on the tape, followed a fraction of a second later by the video image being recorded on the same part of the tape. Clever recording and replay techniques ensure the two signals are recovered independently from the tape, with no interference between them, just as PDP models of memory respond to distinct cues and provide unique responses to them.

4.3   An example of a PDP model of learning and memory

McClelland and Rumelhart (1986) used a PDP model based closely on the example in Techniques Box N to demonstrate the behaviour of a distributed model of memory. The network was expanded from 3 to 24 units, and the model was slightly modified in that the output of a unit was calculated from the input by a *squashing function*, rather than simply copied without change. The main result of this 'squashing' function is that output activity of a unit is *constrained*: it is forced to remain between −1 and +1. As a corollary of this, all input patterns were forced to be patterns of −1 and +1. These constraints don't affect the general characteristics of the model: they are chiefly implementation details. The function also had a 'decay' factor which tended to reduce the output activation of a unit: this means presentations of an input pattern tend to force the network to 'forget' what it has learned about other patterns. In this model the input calculation (see Tables 3.1 and 3.2) was modified to include the external input pattern, which was simply added to the sum of the activity from the other units. To be precise, in this model the weights are changed to make the difference between the total input and the external input (from the pattern) as small as possible.

McClelland and Rumelhart used this model to demonstrate several characteristics of memory. In each demonstration, several input patterns, designed to represent concepts in the real world, are presented to the network, which learns from each one, using a learning procedure just like the one presented in Techniques Box N. After learning, the network is cued with pattern fragments, and the output response is interpreted to see if it corresponds with the input patterns.

Learning a prototype from exemplars
The first demonstration was designed to model the situation when someone (e.g. a child) sees a number of different exemplars of a concept, such as a dog, and learns the meaning of a concept without ever seeing the 'pure' concept on its own, as it were: only particular individuals are seen. There are many prototype-based theories of concept formation, and a short introduction to them can be found in Eysenck and Keane (1990, p. 263). The main idea is that categories are organized around a *prototype*, to which all the exemplars are related to a greater or lesser degree. For some psychological models the prototype is a distinct entity, an abstraction which comprises the most typical properties (e.g. see Rosch, 1978). Exemplars of the concept are compared with the prototype in order to determine whether they are members of the category. The models can be refined in such a way that what is abstracted is not so much a 'perfect' exemplar, but instead a collection of salient attributes or features, which if present in an exemplar lead to its categorization as one of the concepts. The main alternative to prototype theory is the view that psychological concepts consist of the collections of exemplars which make them up (e.g. Medin and Schaffer, 1978; Hintzman, 1986). In this case, there is no distinct entity which is the prototype, but simply the collection of exemplars. According to prototype theory, the concept of dog is represented as an abstraction made up of the most typical dog properties: while the alternative view has the concept of dog represented mentally by the collection of different dog exemplars.

Whichever form these theories take, they all have the psychological problem of how the concept is created, since people never see the 'abstract' concept itself. Rather, all they experience is a set of individual examples. For many concepts, it's hard to imagine what a perfect prototype could be: consider the concept 'furniture', for instance. So it would be most interesting to see what a PDP network, designed to learn from input patterns in the way set out above, makes of a whole series of individual exemplars, and whether it can respond to them as a category in a meaningful way.

McClelland and Rumelhart (1986) explored this with an auto-associative network of 24 units. The model divided up the input pat-

Table 3.5   Examples of three input patterns to McClelland and Rumelhart's auto-associative network

Examples of 'individual name'	Examples of 'individual dog' part (such as in real life)
+ + + − − − + + (Fido)	+ − + − − + − + + + + + + − − − (Cocker Spaniel)
+ − + + − + − + (Rover)	+ − + + − − − − + − + − + − − − (Alsatian)
− − + − + + + − (Spot)	+ − − + − − + − − + + − + − − − (Poodle)

tern over the 24 units into a pattern over the first 8 units, which is set up to 'represent' the name of an individual dog (e.g. Fido, Rover, etc.) and so will differ completely on each presentation (we are pretending the child sees each individual dog once only). The last 16 units are the 'representation' of an individual dog (i.e. the dog itself), rather like a collection of features. Three examples of input patterns are shown in Table 3.5. The 'name' parts of these individual patterns, over the first 8 units, are all quite different: they are uncorrelated. This is intended to reflect the fact that names of dogs (Fido, Rover) are arbitrary and don't have features in common. However, the patterns of the last 16 units in each exemplar, the 'dog' part, are similar to the other exemplars: they are correlated. This is intended to mimic the fact that various dogs do have similar features because they are not arbitrary objects. Dogs have four legs, two eyes, etc., and also more unique 'doggy' attributes such as tail-wagging and barking. In fact, each pattern is a slight distortion of the pattern which is defined as the dog 'prototype'. The 'prototype' of the dog was defined as the following pattern of 16 inputs, described only by their sign (remember inputs had to be +1 or −1):

(+ − + + − − − − + + + + + − − −)

This is, if you like, the representation of the abstract 'typical' dog. So each individual 'dog' pattern was created by distorting this prototype by 'flipping' each unit's sign (from + to − or vice versa) with a small probability (0.2). The result is that each individual instance of 'dog' was based on or similar to the prototype pattern above, with a few (between 2 and 7) of the 16 units 'flipped'. Flipping a unit might be similar to seeing some dogs with black ears and some with white. The name pattern over units 1–8 was entirely random in each case. The network was presented with 50 different 'dogs', each with a new random name, and a new distortion of the prototype. It was expected that the units involved in the 'dog' representation would have strong connections because the 'individual dogs' presented were correlated, while the units involved in the 'name' part would not be strongly connected because the names were not correlated.

The network was indeed found to produce strong connections between the 16 units which were part of the 'dog' representation, and weak connections between the 8 'name' units. It also responded most strongly to the presentation of the original dog prototype itself, despite the fact that the prototype was a 'stimulus' or input pattern it never experienced during learning.

SAQ 24
When a network responds most strongly to a stimulus which is an abstraction from many individual stimuli, what is this property called?

So the model seems to be capable of generating for itself a representation of the original (but never seen) prototype. More interesting is the model's behaviour when more than one prototype was presented. Two new prototypes were created for the concepts 'cat' and 'bagel', again using 16 units:

cat: $(+ - + + - - - - + - + - + + - +)$
bagel: $(+ + - + - + + - + - - + + + + -)$

These additional prototypes were chosen so that the cat, being a small mammal, shared some 'features' with the dog prototype: in fact its correlation with the dog prototype is 0.5. It wouldn't share the more 'doggy' attributes (e.g. barking) however. The bagel, however, is not correlated with either of the other prototypes. McClelland and Rumelhart were interested in the capability of the network to learn three different prototypes simultaneously, of which two were related to each other to a certain extent.

In this case the prototypes themselves were given prototype 'names' (e.g. 'cat', 'dog' or 'bagel'); that is, for each of the three prototypes a unique pattern was defined over the first 8 units which was always paired with the individual examples of that prototype. In other words, the 'name' part of the pattern did not vary randomly but was designed to see if the network could learn to associate three predefined, fixed name patterns with an abstraction derived from the presented individual distortions of the three prototypes (see Table 3.6). As before, 50 different distortions of each prototype pattern were presented, along with

Table 3.6

Name pattern (does not change when presented)		Original prototype representation (distorted when presented)
+ − + − + − + −	(Dog)	+ − + + − − − − + + + + + − − −
+ + − − + + − −	(Cat)	+ − + + − − − − + − + − + + − +
+ − − + + − − +	(Bagel)	+ + − + − + + − + − − + + + + −

the appropriate, undistorted prototype name pattern, to the network (for a total of 150 presentations of exemplars). Once again, the network was never presented with the actual prototype patterns.

Table 3.7 shows the results of testing the network by cueing with parts of the patterns, either using just the name part or the prototype part of the pattern in order to see if the network responds with the rest of the appropriate pattern. The first section shows that presentation of the dog 'name' pattern as cue produces a response pattern which accurately reflects the 'dog' prototype pattern, and vice versa for cueing with the 'dog' prototype pattern. The results for the other two patterns are equally good, as Table 3.7 shows. These results simulate a human's ability to recognize that individual cats, dogs and bagels are examples of the general concepts cat, dog and bagel.

This is an especially interesting result for the dog and cat prototypes, whose prototype patterns were correlated. It shows that a PDP network accurately learns to discriminate three prototypes from the presentation of many individual exemplars, all different. And the network has no idea, prior to or during learning, how many prototypes lie behind the individuals it is presented with, nor is it informed at presentation how 'good' an exemplar each stimulus is. The underlying prototype structure is derived from commonalities in the input pat-

Table 3.7 Results of tests after learning the dog, cat, and bagel patterns (adapted from McClelland and Rumelhart, 1986, p. 186)

	Name pattern	Prototype pattern
Original pattern for dog	+ − + − + − + −	+ − + + − − − + + + + + − − −
Response to dog name	*Dog name presented as cue*	+ − + + − − − + + + + + − − −
Response to dog prototype	+ − + − + − + −	*Dog prototype presented as cue*
Original pattern for cat	+ + − − + + − −	+ − + + − − − + − + − + + − +
Response to cat name	*Cat name presented as cue*	+ − + + − − − + − + − + + − +
Response to cat prototype	+ + − − + + − −	*Cat prototype presented as cue*
Original pattern for bagel	+ − − + + − − +	+ + − + − + + − + − − + + + + −
Response to bagel name	*Bagel name presented as cue*	+ + − + − + + − + − − + + + + −
Response to bagel prototype	+ − − + + − − +	*Bagel prototype presented as cue*

terns as an automatic consequence of learning by error propagation (see Section 4.1).

Learning specific and general information simultaneously
Even more impressive is McClelland and Rumelhart's final demonstration. In this, they wanted to see if the model could simultaneously learn a general prototype and specific exemplars. Suppose a child has a neighbour with a dog called Rover, a grandmother with a dog called Fido, and also sees several other unspecified dogs in the park, which are identified as dogs. Will the child (or rather the network!) learn to associate both the specific and the general concepts in this case so that he or she can recognize that dogs are dogs, and also recognize and name Fido and Rover correctly, with no prior knowledge?

The situation uses three different 'name' patterns: one each for 'Fido', 'Rover', and the class name 'dog' (see Table 3.8). The individual 'dog' patterns for Fido and Rover are two particular distortions of the prototype 'dog' pattern. In addition to being presented with these particular Fido and Rover patterns several times (these patterns have repeated

Table 3.8 Results of tests using prototype and specific individual patterns. The bracketed signs are the points where the specific examplars (Fido and Rover) differ from the dog prototype (adapted from McClelland and Rumelhart, 1986, p. 191)

	Name pattern	Prototype pattern
Pattern for dog prototype	+ − + − + − + −	+ − + + − − − + + + + + − − −
Response to prototype name	*Dog name presented as cue*	+ − + + − − − + + + + + − − −
Response to prototype	+ − + − + − + −	*Dog prototype presented as cue*

	Name pattern	Individual pattern
Pattern for Fido individual	+ − − − + − − −	+ − (−) + − − − − + + + + + (+) − −
Response to Fido name	*Specific Fido name presented as cue*	+ − − + − − − − + + + + + + − −
Response to Fido	+ − − − + − − −	*Specific Fido pattern presented as cue*

	Name pattern	Individual pattern
Pattern for Rover individual	+ − − + + + − +	+ (+) + + − − − − + + + + + − − −
Response to Rover name	*Specific Rover name presented as cue*	+ + + + − − − − + + + + + − − −
Response to Rover	+ − − + + + − +	*Specific Rover pattern presented as cue*

presentations, the child 'sees' Fido and Rover many times), the network is presented with several other (non-repeated) different distortions of the dog prototype (the child sees many other dogs once only), as before, making a total of 50 pattern presentations. The other distortions, which were not considered to be particular dogs such as Fido and Rover, were paired with the 'dog' name pattern.

Table 3.8 shows the results. Cueing with the 'dog' name pattern or prototype 'dog' pattern produces the appropriate prototype pattern response (first section). Yet cueing with specific Fido or Rover name patterns produces recall of the appropriate specific Fido or Rover 'dog' pattern and vice versa. The sensitivity of this distributed memory system is indicated by the fact that the Rover 'dog' pattern differs from the 'dog' prototype at only one point (bracketed in the table), yet recall of the name from it as cue (and its recall from the name as cue) is essentially perfect.

So a distributed memory system such as this, learning simply from a set of individual exemplars presented to it, can simultaneously learn specific information about the exemplars and automatically generalize (*spontaneously generalize*) across those exemplars to extract knowledge about prototypes. It can learn and store many different patterns simultaneously in the same network, using one set of connections. It is this multiple use for a single set of connections, over which several different knowledge patterns are distributed, which makes PDP models stand out from other approaches. Procedural models such as ACT* can be made to generalize across stimuli and are designed to perform pattern matching, but the knowledge of the instances in ACT* is not distributed over a single storage system. Furthermore, the interrogation of the PDP network by the cue produced a single response pattern in one process: as if all stored patterns had been processed in parallel to produce the appropriate response. In no sense were the individual stored patterns examined one-by-one for the best fit. The model performs true parallel distributed processing. It is not simply a categorizer or prototype extraction device; it is a much more general memory processor capable of powerful and flexible processing.

This model also gives an interesting insight into the semantic/episodic memory distinction (see Part I, Section 6). The specific information about individual dogs (i.e. each one's name and perhaps where it was seen) is analogous to memory for individual 'episodic' events, while the ability to generalize over those individuals so as to classify them all as dogs is an operation associated with semantic memory. This single PDP processor is capable of learning the specific and the general information simultaneously: episodic and semantic memory operations are combined in the one PDP model. This 'leads naturally to the suggestion that semantic memory may be just the residue of the superposition of episodic traces' (McClelland and Rumelhart, 1986, p. 206). In other words, perhaps in human memory there is no separation of semantic memory from episodic memory, a view which is gaining ground among some psychologists. There are some recent models of memory which attempt to explore this idea systematically (e.g. MINERVA (see Hintzman, 1986)). It does seem that PDP models very much blurr the need for a separation of episodic and semantic memory into two more-or-less independent memory systems.

Summary of Section 4

- PDP networks can learn from input patterns presented to them by a process of gradual modification of connection weights, which are changed in the direction which reduces the error between the network's output and the external input. This process is called learning by *error propagation*.
- The learning process proceeds using purely local information for each connection weight: calculation of the change in weight for one connection does not need information about the error anywhere else in the network.
- Large networks can learn several different patterns simultaneously, storing information about each pattern in one set of weights: the information is *distributed* over all the connection weights.
- The network will respond to 'cueing' with just a part of a pattern by attempting to complete the original pattern. Retrieval of the whole pattern from a fragment of its content is known as *content addressability*.
- When the input patterns being learned are highly correlated, the network can generate the central tendency or prototype which lies behind them, another example of *spontaneous generalization*.
- However, despite this capability for spontaneous generalization, the PDP network's capability to retrieve information from cues (content addressability) means that, given a specific enough cue, it can retrieve the specific information of the individual exemplars from which the prototype generalization is constructed.

5   More powerful PDP models: the simulation of human cognition

The PDP models described above (schema learning, and prototype learning from exemplars) are really 'demonstration' models. They show what these models can do when appropriately configured or trained, and their behaviour is described as simply having various useful characteristics, such as spontaneous generalization and content addressability, which are known to be characteristic of human performance, in a general kind of way. The behaviour of the models, however, is not directly compared with the behaviour of humans in a way that makes a specific comparison with human performance in a given task. PDP models are much more powerful when they attempt to model precisely or *simulate* human performance in a given task. The example we shall now turn to does just that in the field of human reading, by focusing upon the characteristics of the memory store of words which forms the lexicon.

There is enormous psychological interest in the mechanisms of reading. The ability to read and pronounce an enormous corpus of words is clearly a considerable feat of learning and memory. English words with similar letter sequences can have quite different pronunciations: consider *gave-have*, *rose-lose*, *root-soot*, *bomb-comb-womb*. Clearly the rules of pronunciation are quite complex. Words are usually divided into 'regular' words and 'exception' words. Regular words have pronunciations which might be expected from simple rules based on the letter strings within them: words such as *tint*, *gave* and *rose* are regular. Exceptions to these pronunciations would be *pint*, *have* and *lose*. A simple (but not foolproof) way to work out the regular pronunciation of a letter string is to add a letter to make a non-word. Adding *b* to *-ave* produces *bave*, a non-word which is pronounced like *gave*, so we know that is the regular pronunciation.

This ability to pronounce non-words, which generally have never been seen before, means that we haven't just learned a list of all the correct pronunciations for every word we have seen: we must have internalized some mechanism for translating letter strings into pronunciations.

Perhaps there is a way of presenting words, along with their correct pronunciation, to a neural network so that, without any further constraints, the network simply learns the 'rules' of pronunciation and performs word and non-word pronunciation just like we do. However, there is a major qualification, indeed stumbling block, to the models of cognition described in Section 4, based on one-layer auto-associators. They cannot learn to associate patterns which are not *linearly discriminable*. This means that there are some pattern associations which cannot be modelled using one set of linear units, in which the individual inputs are added together simply according to their weights (as described in Techniques Box K). The prototype patterns described in Section 4 could be learned because they were linearly discriminable: they were bound to be because the prototypes were designed to be slightly related (cat and dog) or completely uncorrelated (bagel), and the exemplars were small distortions of these prototypes.

Table 3.9   An example of pattern association which is not linearly predictable

Input	Response
11	0
00	0
10	1
01	1

Table 3.9 shows an example set of pattern associations which are not linearly predictable. Note that the pattern 00 is categorized with its converse 11 (both produce the response 0), and similarly 01 is categorized with 10 (both produce the response 1). The two-layer pattern associator in Figure 3.4 cannot in principle learn this discrimination: there is no set of weights and thresholds which this network can use which would work.

This is because the categorization (00 with 11) versus (01 with 10) cannot be done on the basis of the individual 'features' acting independently (each 'feature' being each 0 or 1 in the pattern), but has to be done on the basis of *combinations* of features. An example of this is the reading of English words. Take the letter string 'ave': the pronunciation of this string can only be determined from its context. A common pronunciation would be as in *gave*. But this differs from the pronunciation found in *have*. Before you think that a simple rule for the pronunciation of 'ave' could be constructed according to the preceding letter (a preceding 'h' means pronounce as in *have*), consider these words: *shave, haven, gavel*. And then how would you cope with *weaver*? Pronunciation of English letter strings comes from a complex analysis of the surrounding word context, sometimes depending on the sentence context itself (consider the two pronunciations — and meanings — of *read*). These analyses cannot be done by simple two-layer pattern associators such as that in Techniques Box K.

5.1   Hidden units

To perform the association shown in Table 3.9 requires an extension to the two-layer pattern associator model. Figure 3.11 shows the model extended to include units placed in between the input and output layers of units. Since these cells receive no direct input (only an input from the bottom layer) and produce no direct output, they are known as *hidden units*. Going back to the 'impossible' associations in Table 3.9, the network in Figure 3.11 performs this association exactly: 00 is categorized with 11 (and produces the associated output 0) while 01 is categorized with 10 (and produces the associated output 1).

156

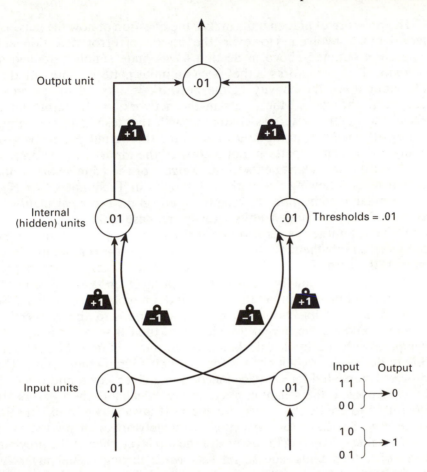

Figure 3.11   A three-layer pattern associator with hidden units (adapted from Rumelhart, Hinton and McClelland, 1986, p. 64)

As indicated in the discussion of Table 3.9, the categorizations (00 with 11) versus (01 with 10) are not *linearly discriminable*: this means that the discrimination can't be done on the basis of individual 'features' acting independently (each 0 and 1 in the pattern), but has to be done on the basis of *combinations* of features. Associations such as these (the reading of English words is an example) can only be handled by using multi-layer networks which include at least one layer of *hidden units*. The 'hidden units' combine the features together to allow the discrimination to be done. Because the hidden units give PDP models considerable extra processing capability, many modern models include them as a matter of course in order to model complex human cognitive capability.

The presence of hidden units makes the question of how the network learns more involved. However, the notion of error detection and correction outlined above in Section 4.1 is quite simply extended to this model. How it works is that once an input pattern is presented to the input units, the activity of the network is allowed to spread or propagate through all the layers in the network to the output units. Then, the output pattern is compared with the desired target output pattern (remember, in a pattern associator the output pattern is generally a new unique pattern, not a copy of the input) and the error is used to calculate adjustments to the weights of the connections in the output layer following the method described in Techniques Box N.

A similar modification of weights based on an error calculation is also used for the hidden units. However, these units, being hidden, don't have a target pattern to aim for: any pattern of output can be produced among them, so the calculation of the error is more involved. In fact, the error for a hidden unit is calculated from the errors previously calculated for the units in the next layer up. For a given connection to a hidden unit, all the errors in the next layer up which arise on that unit's connections are pooled according to the connection weights to create the 'target' for that unit: then that target is used to compare with the input calculation (performed as in Tables 3.1 and 3.2) to derive the weight change for that unit's input connections. The process is repeated for every connection in a given layer, and when all these errors and the weight corrections are calculated, these errors are then used to create the targets for the next layer down in exactly the same way. So the error correction for a network with hidden units relies on first calculating the errors for the top layer, then at the previous layer of hidden units, and so on *backwards* through other layers of hidden units to the input layer, each time basing the new calculation of error on the previous higher layer's error calculation.

This scheme means the computation of new weights *propagates backwards* down the network from the output units to the input units. As this approach is based on the calculation of error in the higher layers, it is known as the *backward propagation of errors* method of learning. One major feature of this learning scheme is that it preserves the situation that the network learns by purely local actions: modification of the weight of any connection is calculated from information local to that connection: that is, the input transmitted from the lower layer unit and the errors in the direct connections above it. The weight calculation requires no knowledge of the state of any part of the network beyond the local connections. In networks with hidden units, this is the dominant mechanism used for creating PDP models capable of learning useful processing capability.

5.2   An example of a powerful multi-level PDP model

We shall now look at a PDP model with hidden units designed to simulate the reading of English words.

Seidenberg and McClelland (1989) set up a PDP model based on a three-layer network with hidden units (see Figure 3.12). 400 'orthographic units' take an input based on letter strings from words. The input is not a simple presentation of individual letters. Instead, the letter strings are encoded as triples, based on a scheme devised by Rumelhart and McClelland (1986). The letter string *make* is represented as the set of letter triples *_ma*, *mak*, *ake*, and *ke_* (the underscore indicates the beginning or end of a word). Furthermore, each individual input unit will respond to a range of different triples. In the scheme used, each unit has a list of 10 possible first letters, 10 possible middle letters and 10 possible final letters. Any letter triple whose first letter corresponds with any letter from the first position list *and* whose second letter corresponds with any letter from the second list, *and* whose final letter corresponds with any letter from the final position list will cause that unit to respond. So each individual unit will respond to many different input triples (1,000 in all). However, as every unit has different letters in its three lists, across the input network of 400 units only a small set of units is excited by a given letter triple. Each triple activates about 20 units in all. It is the different *pattern* of excitement over the 400 input units that uniquely encodes each triple.

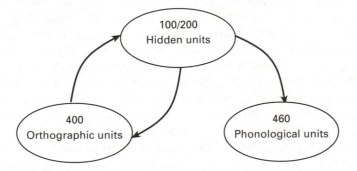

Figure 3.12   Seidenberg and McClelland's (1989) model for word reading (Seidenberg and McClelland, 1989)

This pattern feeds through connections to the hidden units and on to the 460 output 'phonological' units. These have a similar representational scheme, derived from Wickelgren's (1969) triples scheme. Of course, since the aim is to represent phonology (i.e. pronunciation), the encoded features are phonetic ones such as vowel, fricative or stop: the finer details can be found in Rumelhart and McClelland (1986). Once again, however, every output unit responds to a large set of different phoneme triples. However, each phoneme triple corresponds to a unique pattern of excitation of 16 of the 460 output units, so the network as a whole has unique representations for every possible phoneme triple. The important point is that both input and output use distributed representation over many units, so that a given input word, or a given output pronunciation, produces a unique *pattern* of excitation.

After deciding on the representational scheme, some more steps are required before starting on the training process. 2,897 monosyllabic words chosen largely from the Kucera and Francis (1967) word count had to be coded into a computer according to their true pronunciation, and a training regime decided. The network model was to be trained to learn the pronunciations of these words in a way which reflects the uneven experience which we have with English words: the Kucera and Francis word count reveals that the most common word 'the' occurs in English texts over 69,000 times more often than the rare word 'rake'. The training scheme ended up as a set of 150,000 learning trials, in which the most common words appeared 230 times in all, while the least common words were presented about 14 times.

Each of these 150,000 learning trials worked the same way. For the word being 'presented' on that trial, an orthographic string was derived from the letter triples (see the examples for *make* above) and presented as a unique pattern of excitation to the orthographic input units. Activation spreads forward along the connections to the hidden units, which in turn respond and send activation along the second set of connections to the output phonological units. The phonological output units respond to this activity and produce an output pattern or response. This pattern is compared to the previously determined correct phonological definition. Any difference between the network's response and this definitive 'pronunciation' is propagated backwards through the network, and used to adjust all the weights on the connections in such a way that the difference or *error* between what the network produces as a response to the presented 'word' is reduced.

So, after 150,000 learning trials, what has this network learned? The performance of the network is measured by its ability to produce the correct, defined phonology. A measure of this difference is called the *mean squared error*. Figure 3.13 shows how this difference reduces over the course of training. The learning is plotted for four groups of words, as taken from Taraban and McClelland (1987): these are regular or exception words of high or low frequency. Regular words contain letter strings which occur in many words, always with the same pronunciation. For example, *must* contains the sequence *-ust*, which is pronounced the same in other monosyllabic words with that ending (*just*, *dust*, etc.). Exception words are words pronounced differently from the

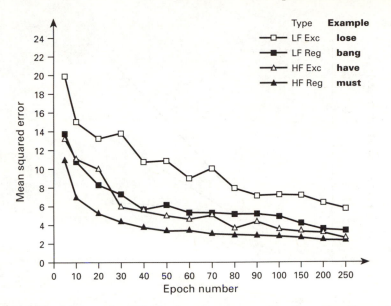

Figure 3.13   Mean phonological error scores for the stimuli used by Taraban and McClelland (based on Taraban and McClelland, 1987)

majority of words with the same letter sequence: *have* is pronounced differently from *gave*, *shave*, *wave*, etc.

Figure 3.13 shows how the network learns the pronunciation of all the words, though even at the end substantial error is found on the low frequency exception words. You can see that regular words and high frequency words give rise to fewer errors. For these words, the network has received a lot more training, presumably in much the same way as humans.

The difference between regular and exception words has been well explored by psychologists interested in reading processes (a good account can be found in Ellis 1993). Psychologists have measured the speed with which people name the words when presented with them (this is known as *naming latency*). Results from an experiment by Waters and Seidenberg (1985) are shown in Figure 3.14. As well as looking at regular and exception words, they looked at 'strange' words: these are words like *corps* or *aisle* which have letter sequences which occur in few other monosyllabic words, and they also have quite idiosyncratic pronunciations. The results for the naming latencies found by Waters and Seidenberg are in the top half of Figure 3.14.

Seidenberg and McClelland's simulation of these results works by presenting to the PDP network the same actual words used by Waters and Seidenberg (1985), and measuring the error in 'pronunciation' after

161

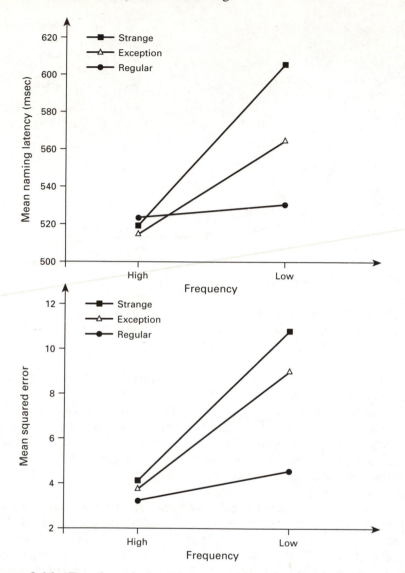

Figure 3.14 Results of the Waters and Seidenberg (1985) studies: experiment (upper graph) and simulation (lower graph) (based on Waters and Seidenberg, 1985)

it had undergone training as described above. This error is the extent to which the phonological output of the network differs from the predetermined correct phonological representation of the word. They assume that this error would somehow be transformed into an effect on naming latency if the model had the capability of transforming the phonological output into actual speech.

The bottom half of Figure 3.14 shows the mean squared error produced by the PDP network for the various groups of words. The type of word and its frequency appear to have much the same effect on the network's error as they do on the naming latency of human subjects. The PDP model appears to be a good *simulation* of human behaviour. Some more results are shown in Figure 3.15. Brown's (1987) experiment used 'unique' words, such as *soap* or *curve*, which have letter sequences not found in other monosyllabic words, but are less eccentric than the 'strange' words and have less idiosyncratic pronunciations.

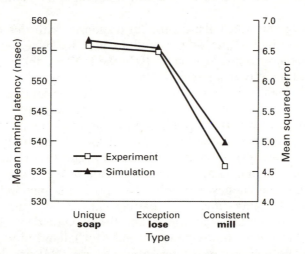

Figure 3.15   Results of Brown (1987): experiment and simulation data (based on Brown, 1987)

Again, the simulation proceeds by presenting the same words used by Brown (1987) to the PDP network and measuring the phonological error. Once again, the type of word has an effect on the network's output error which closely mimics the effects on human naming latency.

Seidenberg and McClelland (1989) explored a whole range of experiments, comparing the naming latency found in human subjects on various groups of words with the error output of their PDP model. By and large, the agreement was very good.

Seidenberg and McClelland do not claim that their PDP model is a complete or final model of the reading process. The most they would want to claim is that the successful simulations show that this approach is probably along the right lines, and is worth pursuing and refining in order to increase its match with behavioural results. Extending the model to allow it to produce actual speech output would also be valuable. The main theoretical contrast they emphasize is with the current psychological theories of human reading. These have concentrated on the likelihood of the existence of several, largely independent, routes which are used to pronounce written words (a simple account can be found in Eysenck and Keane, 1990, pp. 311–17, and a more extended discussion in Ellis, 1993). In such models, regular words are pronounced by using a rule-based system which converts spellings more-or-less directly to sound. However, such a route could not work for exception words, so for these a second route, independent of the first, looks up the meaning of the word in a semantic system (the *semantic lexicon*) which can then be used to look up an unambiguous pronunciation of the word.

Seidenberg and McClelland's model dispenses with this multiplicity of routes, and indeed the simple model which we have looked at dispenses with the semantic lexicon itself. In the PDP model, pronunciation is computed directly from each word's orthography, in a way which is identical for high and low frequency, regular and exception words, and even non-words. The differences found in the naming latencies of these various groups of words are predicted by this single-mechanism model of reading, without recourse to semantic lexicons and multiple routes. At the very least, psychologists wishing to argue that multiple routes are involved in human reading have to provide new evidence, not based simply on naming latency, to justify their position. Such evidence may be based on the impairment to reading caused by brain damage in otherwise healthy adults who were formerly skilled readers (the *acquired dyslexias*). However, the Seidenberg and McClelland model can then attempt to simulate such evidence also. (Ellis (1993) provides a brief account of acquired dyslexias.) There is no doubt that the successful simulation of human behavioural data by PDP network models, even if it does not provide immediate solutions to the analysis of human behaviour, at least presents an enormous challenge to conventional psychological models which must respond if they are to survive.

Summary of Section 5

- Patterns which cannot be discriminated independently on the basis of their simple individual features are not *linearly discriminable*. The discrimination has to be done on the basis of complex combinations of features. A real-life example is the computation of the pronunciation of English words from their orthography (i.e. spellings).
- Pattern associators based on PDP networks can only perform discriminations on stimuli which are not linearly discriminable by incorporating extra layers of computational units. These layers, which have no direct external input and produce no external output, are made up of *hidden units*.

164

- PDP networks with layers of hidden units learn associations by *backward propagation of errors*. The final output of the top layer is compared with the target output, and the error is used to calculate a target for the previous layer, generating a new error each time, and so on backwards down the network.
- A three-layer pattern associator, designed by Seidenberg and McClelland (1989), with an appropriate distributed representational scheme for input orthography (spelling) and output phonology (pronunciation), can learn the correct 'pronunciations' of English words.
- This pattern associator, when trained in the pronunciation of English words, *simulates* the results obtained from psychology experiments which measure human responses to naming various types of words, such as high and low frequency, regular and exception words.
- The successful simulation of human behaviour by a PDP network model which computes its output in a single step, has no built-in rules, and is configured simply by training the network on correct pronunciations challenges conventional psychological models which rely on multiple pronunciation mechanisms, and are frequently dependent on explicitly specified rule-based systems.

6   General issues concerning PDP models

I have introduced the basic elements that lie behind PDP models: single and multi-layer networks, pattern associators and auto-associators, learning by error detection, backward propagation, and the need for hidden units. We've seen that even small networks (tiny in comparison to the number of neurons in the brain) are capable of learning concepts and responding to interrogation by cues in ways at least highly reminiscent of the way in which the human cognitive system operates, using schemas, extracting prototypes, recalling specific concepts, and computing phonology from orthography. How do such models relate to the rest of our understanding of the brain and human cognition?

6.1   Neural networks?

Throughout my description of PDP models, I have deliberately refrained from describing the units in the network as neurons or synapses. Superficially, without examining in any detail the precise neuro-anatomy of the human brain and the various neuron types that are found, models based on units which receive input from a number of other units and broadcast a response to many others over directional connections look like a good starting point for modelling actual neural networks and their behaviour. Even the learning mechanism is based on local operations. Some researchers go so far as to create drawings of their models in which the units have the amoeboid appearance of a stereotypic neuron, and the connections between them are depicted as classical synapses.

In reality, however, the vast majority of these models have little more than this entirely superficial relationship to neural anatomy. While it may be that they, or rather the researchers, were 'neurally inspired', these models are actually mathematically based computational models based on networks of parallel processing computational units. The characteristics of these units are usually derived, not from known characteristics of neuronal function and behaviour, but from known properties of *mathematical* concepts, such as matrix algebra, differential equations, binary logic, and so on. And as soon as you attempt to look at the detailed construction and activity of the human brain, you find the reality down there in those neurons is quite different from the ideal mathematical world of activity functions and linear responses. To cite just one example, so far there is no anatomical evidence of neural networks in which a set of neurons connects to all the others of the same type. Several researchers (Crick and Asanuma, 1986; Smolensky, 1986) have pointed out that PDP models are a long way from being based in neuronal reality.

6.2   Achievements of PDP models

The main achievement of PDP models is to set out a simple mechanism which processes information and learns in ways which possess some of the characteristics of human learning and information processing. Such characteristics are pattern matching, spontaneous generalization, content-addressable memory, stimulus categorization, and concept learning. Many of these characteristics are natural or 'emergent' properties of PDP models. This makes PDP models very attractive to psychologists, who want to explain why human information processing has the characteristics it does. If they can point to the fact that any information processor constructed out of elemental local processors networked together will inevitably possess these emergent properties of PDP models, then at least some aspects of human performance are perhaps explicable in terms of the properties of the neural networks which make up the brain.

Beyond these striking general emergent properties, which characterize all PDP models, researchers are having some success at modelling *specific* aspects of human performance (as we saw in Section 5). A carefully constructed network of simple units, incorporating an elementary coding scheme for orthography and phonology, is capable of learning the pronunciation of English words from many presentations of them, and of doing so in a way which results in a system which closely mimics *details* of human performance measured in a number of psychology experiments, as shown by Figures 3.12 to 3.15. So, in addition to having general properties which appear to explain aspects of human cognition, PDP models provide psychologists with a valuable tool for exploring aspects of human cognition systematically, using ever more sophisticated models.

6.3   Weaknesses of PDP models

There are two main areas of weakness for PDP models. First, there are specific problems with particular models in that they fail to simulate human behaviour exactly. Secondly, there are fundamental problems as to whether neural networks can be sufficiently powerful to be applied to all areas of human cognition, including areas where the rule-based approach has proved successful in the past.

6.4   Inaccuracies in PDP models

All psychological models are imperfect in some way, and PDP models are no exception. There are many facets to human performance, and capturing them all is an enormous task. Consider the Seidenberg and McClelland experiment described in Section 5.2. Despite its success in simulating experimental results of human reading, some aspects of the model's performance were decidedly non-human. For example, some of the errors it made in pronunciation are often made by children learning to read: pronouncing *dose* like *rose*, or *womb* like *comb*. But other errors are almost never encountered in humans: pronouncing *romp* as *ramp*, *bronze* as *branz*, and worse *zip* as *vip*, *taps* as *tats*. So the model is not so accurate as to be an exact mirror of human performance. These kinds of problems, though, are all grist to the mill and serve to encourage psychologists to try to improve on PDP models in order to cope with discrepancies.

A potentially more serious problem is with the learning sequence. Seidenberg and McClelland's model was given 150,000 learning trials in which words were presented to the network and it learned from the error in its pronunciation. A common objection to PDP models is that humans can learn much faster than that, and that in a case like this just a few, or even one, presentation of the word with the correct pronunciation can be enough for learning.

Of course, the 150,000 trials weren't needed to learn just one word's pronunciation: they were needed for the whole set of 2,897 words. Even the most common word only appeared a total of 230 times, the least common a mere 14 times. Seidenberg and McClelland might answer that these numbers of presentations could well be considerable *underestimates* of the amount of experience that children get with words as they grow up, and that perhaps it was remarkable that their network had learnt so much with as *few* as 150,000 presentations. However, one area of learning with which current PDP models cope very badly is *one-trial learning*. It is probable (at least in the case of reasonably proficient readers) that being told the pronunciation of a new word just once is enough to guarantee perfect performance in the future. Attempts at modelling the kind of single-trial learning that are abundant in countless experiments in memory have so far been very unsuccessful. The problem with our current account of learning in PDP networks is that it relies on the slow reduction of output error by gradually converging the connection strengths in the network on the ideal solution. This gradual error reduction seems fundamentally incompatible with the idea of one-trial learning. Thus, for PDP models to successfully capture this behaviour, either an alternative learning scheme has to be invented which acts much faster than the existing mechanism, or alternatively new architectures of interacting PDP networks must be created which are specifically aimed at reproducing one-trial learning. An early example of this is J.A. Anderson's network model for memorizing short serial lists (Anderson, 1973). In this area, too, it is hoped that the problems with the models are ones which can be addressed by further developments, and do not represent fundamental limits to the application of PDP models beyond which they cannot be used.

6.5   Are there aspects of human cognition to which the PDP approach cannot be applied?

A more accurate phrasing of this question might be: are there human cognitive processes for which PDP models are an inappropriate level of analysis? If this is the case, then there must be fundamental restrictions upon the capability of purely PDP-based models which mean that they cannot, *by themselves*, form a *complete* account of human cognitive behaviour. This question is currently a source of intense controversy, with psychologists taking up positions in at least three, if not more, camps. The controversy arises because any claim to universality by adherents of PDP models (and such a claim is generally made implicitly, rather than explicitly) brings the approach into direct conflict with the rule-based approach to cognitive modelling, which previously pretended to the throne of universality.

An example of the battleground is in linguistics. Even the elementary skill of learning to read English words, modelled by Seidenberg and McClelland with a PDP network, is one that formerly would have been modelled by a rule-based system in which general rules of converting letter sequences to pronunciations were modified by more and more specific rules to cope with irregular cases. The conflict rapidly escalates as the PDP approach takes a closer interest in the subject matter of linguistics itself: that is, the nature of well-formed sentences and the grammar which may, or may not, lie behind them. The enormous regularities in human language have led linguists to capture that regularity in *rules* of grammar, which can be used to define what are, and what are not, valid sentences. Modern generative grammars, following Chomsky, use a rule-based approach to define 'the form of knowledge which is put to use in linguistic behaviour' (Kuroda, 1987, p. 7; see also Eysenck and Keane, 1990, pp. 318–21). To linguists and many psycholinguists, rule-governed behaviour seems to lie at the heart of human language.

However, the PDP adherent, while entirely accepting that language can be *summarized* by a grammatical system based on rules, claims that the regularities in human language arise from the general properties of parallel distributed processors *in which there are no explicit rules underlying the linguistic performance of humans*.

As a result, 'linguistic rules therefore lose their causal role in cognition, an unacceptable outcome [to linguists] . . . the fundamental objection is to the loss of rules as an explanatory device' (Bechtel and Abrahamsen, 1991, p. 295). The threat of the replacement of rules as the explanation of highly regular linguistic behaviour by the perhaps capricious behaviour of unprincipled neural networks is one that cannot be ignored.

The strongest objection to the universal application of PDP models to cognition comes from Fodor and Pylyshyn (1988). In an elaborate and complex argument, they attempt to prove that there are aspects of human cognition which in principle can only be modelled by rule-based systems, and hence for which the PDP approach is inadequate. Fodor and Pylyshyn are especially critical of the *representational* power of PDP models. One of the criticisms of the Seidenberg and McClelland model of reading is the inadequacy and essential arbitrariness of the representational scheme, despite its apparent complexity. Fodor and Pylyshyn claim that the PDP approach is inadequate for its task of representation. One example they use comes from language, and is the representation of the sentence *Joan loves the florist*. In a PDP model, they argue, the network will provide patterns of activity for *Joan*, *loves*, and *florist*, and an association between them, but this representation will be fundamentally incapable of discriminating this sentence from *The florist loves Joan*. Adding representations concerning relationships would disambiguate the sentence in terms of semantics, but would not capture the syntactic structure (viz. that Joan is the subject).

In the rule-based approach, however, the syntactic relationships are automatically captured by the grammar rules, so there is no chance of confusion between the sentences. Further, the syntactic relationship between the two sentences is automatically captured, a feat of which the PDP representation is fundamentally incapable, so 'there must be something deeply wrong with Connectionist [=PDP] architectures' (Fodor and Pylyshyn, 1988, p. 49).

Although more recent PDP architectures (e.g. Pollack's RAAM, 1990) begin to address these problems, Fodor and Pylyshyn's other arguments make a strong case for the rule-based account in cognitive models. The most common means of reconciling the conflicting views is to fall back on the concept of levels. The idea of explaining things at all kinds of levels is how we approach many complex issues. Even a washing machine can be understood in many ways. A molecular view of it would explain the motion of electrons along interconnecting conductors and the general motion of water and soap molecules as they are heated and tumbled; an energy field level of explanation would consider the creation of magnetic fields to spin the motor and the use of drum rotation to tumble the clothes and spin them dry. At the higher levels are the more familiar descriptions of washing machine operation: putting in clothes and detergent, filling with water and going through the operations of washing, rinsing and spin drying. PDP models explain certain memory phenomena at a different level from that of the rule-based approach. These low-level explanations derive from the *emergent properties* of PDP models based on simple local computations in networks of elementary elements. We know that human memory shows properties such as content addressability and spontaneous generalization. If we can show that all PDP models, by their very nature, will show these properties, and we can satisfy ourselves that the human brain is an example of a PDP network, then we have a good explanation of why human memory has those properties: they are inevitable given a human memory system implemented in a PDP architecture (a true neural network).

However, this apparent explanatory strength of PDP modelling is also exploited by its opponents as a weakness. These emergent properties tend to be very *low-level* phenomena: they are elementary aspects of human memory and cognition, such as content-addressable memory and low-level perception. There has been little success in discovering examples of such emergent properties for functions of *high-level* cognition, such as language and problem solving. Furthermore, rule-based systems can themselves display emergent properties. An example is one called AM, which was given a 'scanty knowledge of a hundred elementary concepts of finite set theory' (Lenat, 1977, p. 839). This system explored elementary number theory and came up with a number of discoveries for itself (these discoveries were known facts about numbers which were *not* built-in). The new facts 'emerged' from the application of heuristic rules to a given knowledge base, resulting in new knowledge. This capability of the discovery of mathematical truths seems to be at a higher level than the kind of emergent properties found in PDP models. Fodor and Pylyshyn (1988), although they criticize heavily the utility of PDP models as a usable modelling system, happily acknowledge that the human brain, which would presumably implement the rule-based cognitive systems which they wish to pursue, is almost certainly a massively parallel distributed processing machine. But according to them PDP models are not an appropriate *level* at which to base explanations of high-level cognition: they are *merely* accounts of the low-level implementation of a rule-based system of cognition.

The accent is on the *mere* of merely implementations. Fodor and Pylyshyn argue that the low-level implementation of cognitive models is of no relevance to the models themselves. By appealing to examples from the rest of science, they claim that the explanations found at one level of a structure are irrelevant to other levels: for example, the explanations of atomic physics aren't much use to a biochemist studying genetic engineering. The explanations of a washing machine at the molecular level are of little use for anyone doing the family washing. According to this view, PDP models are 'no more relevant to theories of cognition than are stories about molecular processes in the brain' (Bechtel and Abrahamsen, 1991).

Fodor and Pylyshyn also go further and say that, although low-level properties of cognition (such as content addressability) are better explained by PDP models, when a new generation of computers based on PDP appears, then a rule-based system actually implemented on a PDP network will also display those low-level properties, since they result from the (mere) implementation. Rule-based systems don't display those low-level properties now because historically they have so far been implemented on conventional digital ('von Neumann') computers. In this sense, these properties of PDP systems (generalization, associative memory, even schema-based recall) are inevitable for a cognitive system implemented in PDP hardware (a real 'neural network'), rather than necessary features of cognitive systems in general.

Needless to say, PDP researchers are not easily discouraged. In particular, just because rule-based systems appear to enjoy success in modelling some cognitive systems, it doesn't mean they are the *only* way to do it. The challenge for PDP modelling is to create simulations which 'account for the phenomena that are handled rather well by rules but also, without additional mechanisms, give an elegant account of other phenomena as well' (Bechtel and Abrahamsen, 1991, p. 217). How many psychological phenomena can be explained by PDP models, how many will require a rule-based approach, and what new theories will be devised are all questions for the future.

To summarize this view, certain (low-level) aspects of human cognition, such as pattern matching, content-addressable memory, and schema-based processing fall naturally in a domain that lends itself to PDP modelling. Other aspects, such as problem solving, playing chess, perhaps using language, may be at too high a level for the PDP approach even to be applied, still less to show some success, but can be modelled using a rule-based approach. The result is that human cognition is carved up into areas which are best treated by one, or the other, approach. However, there has been some success in modelling problem solving with PDP models, and there is great interest in many quarters (including industry) in the possibility of using PDP models for natural language processing. So at the boundaries furious battles ensue. PDP adherents are currently hammering on the door of linguistic performance, expecting it to cave in at any moment, while grammarians steadfastly barricade the door against encroachment by the network anarchists who wish to deny the rule (of rules!).

Finally, there is one outcome of the rise of PDP modelling which is quite rare. In Section 1, I pointed out how cognitive models had been largely inspired by existing technology, leading up to the development of the rule-based approach. Dogged pursuance of PDP models for the last fifty years has finally paid off in the other direction, inspiring new developments in computer architecture. Invariably and incorrectly called 'neural networks' (they are, of course, manufactured using silicon chips), the new generation of computers may perhaps lead to the development of artificial intelligence which is far nearer to human intelligence than anything we know of today.

Summary of Section 6

- PDP models bear a resemblance to networks based on real neurons, but real neurons have characteristics quite different from the processing units in PDP models.
- PDP models have largely been developed from a background of known mathematical devices, such as matrix algebra and calculus.
- The rule-based approach, with its reliance on explicit rules, contrasts most strongly with PDP models. PDP models have no explicitly defined rule-based system.
- The natural (or 'emergent') properties of PDP networks may provide an explanation of certain characteristics of human performance, especially in memory tasks.
- The PDP approach can be used as a general system for modelling and simulating human cognitive behaviour.
- Inaccuracies and incapabilities in PDP models (such as their inability to perform one-trial learning) should lead to the development of new learning techniques or innovative PDP architectures.
- PDP models cannot, at present, by themselves form a universal account of human cognition. There is considerable doubt as to whether such universality is possible.
- However, aspects of human performance which appear so regular as to be conveniently summarized by rules (like the rules of grammar in language), may arise from the general properties of parallel distributed processors, which in fact operate without any reference to such rules.
- Nevertheless, some aspects of human cognition may require a rule-based approach to modelling. Various levels of human cognition may be best described either by one or the other approach. It remains to be seen where the future boundaries between the rule-based approach and PDP modelling lie.

Further reading

Chapter 7 of *Connectionism and the Mind* (Bechtel and Abrahamsen, 1991) offers an especially good analysis of critiques of PDP and responses to those critiques.

Chapter 7 of *Parallel Distributed Processing* (Morris, 1989) extends the Seidenberg and McClelland model presented here, and Chapter 8 presents a forceful critique of PDP models.

Overview
Martin Le Voi

1 Phenomena and cognition

This book falls neatly into two halves. The first half (Part I and Part IIA) concentrates on memory phenomena, presenting the evidence to show how human memory performs in real life. We see how people respond to cues, how they abstract and generalize information, how they can be misled by leading questions, how limited memory capacity influences performance. These are the natural *phenomena* of human memory, which must be accurately documented and analysed by laboratory experimentation or careful fieldwork, before useful theories can be developed, refined and sometimes rejected in the light of new findings about human memory which are inconsistent with them. The aspects of memory documented here are not an exhaustive survey of all memory phenomena; many more can be found in other textbooks and articles. They do illustrate, however, how the discovery and documentation of the characteristics of memory drive psychologists on to the construction of theories. The methods of investigation used were aimed mainly at data-gathering, either by regular laboratory experimental procedures (such as presenting constructed scenarios of accidents for eye-witnesses to recall, or asking people to perform two tasks at once in working memory experiments), or by naturalistic observational techniques (such as diary studies).

In the second half of the book (Part IIB and Part III), there is no attempt to discover and document further characteristics of memory. Instead, the aim is to derive *general* models of human cognition which, it is hoped, will increase our *understanding* of how memory works. So, rather than just a list of what memory does when you do this or try that, we also need to have some idea of the role of memory within the human cognitive system. Here the methods are based on constructing computational models in a computing system (either rule-based or a 'neural net') and using these to construct large-scale simulations of human cognitive behaviour.

2 Theories and explanations

The first half of this book is not completely devoid of theory, however. In fact, it is not really possible even to describe memory phenomena, much less research them, without having a reasonably firm theoretical base. Let's take a few characteristics of memory. We know that human memory selects, abstracts, integrates and normalizes information (Part I, Section 3.3). Inconsistent information may be forgotten, while consistent information may be generated at recall even if it didn't happen! All these *various* phenomena (and more) can be conveniently summarized by a *single* theory: schema theory. We theorize that human memory operates by means of general purpose schemas which organize storage and retrieval of information in a particular way, and that this is the cause of the memory phenomena which we have documented. There is an intimate relation between the theory and the phenomena, and because schema theory captures many different facts about memory, we follow a long tradition and claim that this theory is an *explanation* of those characteristics. Of course, it may not be the only possible explanation, or even the best one, but if one theory accurately describes several disparate facts (Isaac Newton called this 'saving the phenomena') we can propose it as an explanation.

A second example of the use of theory comes in Part IIA: the theory and characteristics of working memory. The phenomena are really quite simple: we can't remember more than about seven chunks with complete accuracy in the short term; we can remember more short words than long words; it's hard to do two things at once especially when they are very similar in some way. By careful experimentation we are able to document these characteristics with considerable accuracy, so we can be quite precise, for example, about when two tasks are so similar that they interfere. We can then construct a theory which captures all these phenomena with a convenient summary based on multiple co-operating working memory systems (see Figure 2.2 in Part IIA). Again, the intimate connection between this theory and the various phenomena to which it is applied allows us to advance it as an explanation of those memory characteristics.

3   Models and simulation

In the second half of this book (Parts IIB and III), the focus turns away from looking at the fine details of how memory works. Instead of devising a theory of memory to explain a few characteristics found in a small range of experiments, the research described here acknowledges the fact that memory is an integral part of the whole cognitive system and cannot be treated in isolation. The second half of the book is concerned with attempts to create systems capable of application not only to memory, but also to problem solving, linguistic behaviour, perception, etc. The aim is to *unify* theories over all areas of human cognition.

Anderson's approach is to come up with a general-purpose cognitive architecture, or system, which can be used to develop ideas in all areas of human cognition (see Part IIB, Figure 2.5). Such a framework allows psychologists to develop general models of aspects of human cognition, such as memory or problem solving. These models are useful devices for exploring ideas about these cognitive systems and how they relate to each other. Whereas theories are designed specifically for explaining the specific results of a number of experiments, models are used to test ideas about the various cognitive systems in a much more general way. They are not aimed directly at explanation, and are not specific enough to lend themselves to a critical empirical test. This is expecially true of rule-based systems, which can be programmed to model anything. Because of the enormous capabilities of models programmed to run on computer systems, it is very difficult to devise experiments which may lead to rejection of the whole cognitive framework.

Within a modelling framework, such as Anderson's ACT*, systems can be built up which attempt to recreate human cognitive phenomena, such as generalization in memory, or problem-solving behaviour. These attempts to mimic human performance can be thought of as *simulations*. These simulations can be compared directly with human performance, thereby producing some interesting insights into the constraints and capabilities of human cognition. This comparison forms the main basis of tests of the models, though it is the simulations which are under direct test, rather than the cognitive architecture itself.

Rule-based systems like ACT* are not the only architectures for deriving models of human cognition. PDP models also provide an architecture for modelling memory as being made up of interconnected networks of simple individual processors. Seidenberg and McClelland devised a model within this architecture (see Part III, Section 5.2) and used it to simulate the human performance of reading single words. The output of the simulation can be compared directly with human performance, and its successes and failures examined to help psychologists produce better models in the future. If human performance differs markedly from performance predicted by the simulation, it is necessary to consider ways of improving the model, focusing attention on aspects of cognition which we still do not understand.

4 Conclusion

Progress in psychology, therefore, is based on a judicious mixture of, on the one hand, careful investigation of the characteristics of human cognition generally using either naturalistic or empirical data-gathering techniques, and, on the other hand, careful development of large-scale computational models which simulate human behaviour of all kinds. Within these fields, this book has only been able to cover a small area of the work in progress. Large areas of research in psychology have had to be omitted, such as the developmental approach which looks at how human memory develops through childhood and deteriorates through aging. Another area of great interest is cognitive neuro-psychology, which looks at how normal human cognition is affected by abnormal situations in the brain, such as failure to grow and develop properly, or actual damage through accident, disease or surgery. Such an approach can be very revealing if a highly specific alteration in brain structure produces a related specific loss of function: sometimes a function may not be identifiable until its loss reveals the importance it plays in overall human cognition. Eysenck and Keane (1990, pp. 503–6) explore the usefulness of this approach, and indeed integrate it with much of their discussion of cognitive psychology.

In general, it's important to appreciate that a fuller understanding of psychology comes from casting the widest net possible, and taking account of evidence from all areas of theoretical and empirical research. PDP models seem to be an elementary associative memory system, yet they may shed light on the construction of schema-based models, and also other aspects of cognition such as learning to read words aloud. The construction of working memory systems as explanations of various characteristics of performance grows both from empirical work with laboratory tasks and the development of large-scale rule-based computer models like ACT*. These approaches are not alternative or competing ways to study psychology: they are the two sides of the same coin.

Answers to SAQs

SAQ 1
(a) and (b) should be accessible to introspection because they are fairly slow processes with several component steps. (c) is so automatic and (d) so instantaneous that there is little or no conscious insight into the processes involved. (e) may sometimes involve a slow search or processes of trial and error that can be reported, but sometimes the solution just 'pops up' and the solver has no idea what processes produced it.

SAQ 2
Cooker, sink and teapot would have high schema expectancy in a kitchen and would be most likely to be remembered. Hat and stethoscope would have low schema expectancy and would be less likely to be recalled. Items like pots and pans, that are very probable objects in a kitchen, might be falsely recalled if they were not actually present.

SAQ 3
Group A tend to give a higher estimate of the speed. Their judgment is influenced by the word 'smashed', which implies greater impact and higher speed.

SAQ 4
(a) A confusion or blend: confusing the objects involved in the actions.
(b) A reversal: component actions wrongly ordered.
(c) A goal switch.

SAQ 5
(a) and (c) are semantic knowledge; (b) and (d) are episodic knowledge. (a) and (c) are general factual statements; (b) and (d) contain specific details, and refer to a specific occasion.

SAQ 6
The answer is (b), because in this condition people can make use of previous knowledge to reduce the memory load. Most people would not have known the trade deficit figures for 1975 so (c) does not help.

SAQ 7
Generally speaking, adults have a greater memory span than children. In part, this reflects greater verbal skills, but more importantly the fact that chunking enhances memory span usually gives adults a greater advantage.

SAQ 8
(a) Phonological store, central executive, possibly articulatory control system.
(b) Articulatory control system.
(c) Possibly all four components.

SAQ 9
Firstly, the attentional resources of the central executive would be required. Since the problems are presented visually, the visuospatial sketchpad might be involved. Finally, the fact that the task involves verbal material where the order of the letters is important suggests the likely use of the articulatory control system.

Answers to SAQs

SAQ 10
Add *Production rule 1a*:
Condition: IF your goal is to make a cup of tea but you have no tea
Action: THEN activate the goal of buying tea
Modify *Production rule 2*:
Condition: IF you have a goal of buying milk or tea and you have enough money
Action: THEN go to the shop
Add *Production rule 3a*:
Condition: IF you are in the shop and your goal is to buy tea
Action: THEN say 'Can I have a packet of tea please!'

SAQ 11
1 Declarative (just a static fact).
2 Procedural (it is really a procedure that can be executed).
3 Procedural (notice that it is a production rule).
4 Declarative (for you, although procedural for the *fox*!).
5 Ambiguous. This has both a procedural reading: 'Add two and two together to get four'; and a declarative reading: it is a fact that 'Two and two is four'.

SAQ 12
1 The home which sends out more calls than it receives.
2 The homes that receive the most calls (or more than some threshold value).

SAQ 13
1 Working memory.
2 Procedural and declarative memory.
3 Tangled hierarchies in declarative memory.
4 Action parts of rules.
5 Hierarchical goal structures.
6 Condition–action pairings in rules.

SAQ 14
1 A pencil.
2 A paper knife.
3 The stem of a spectacle frame.
4 A rolled-up piece of paper (debatable, since it might go so limp that it cannot be used for stirring; or it may have unpleasant-tasting ink on it).

SAQ 15
(a) Probably
(b) The general concept of 'grandmother' would be represented by another single cell: the brain cannot know whether what is represented is a physical object (person) or an abstracted concept.
(c) If the cell for recognition of your grandmother died, presumably you would be unable to recognize her.

SAQ 16
When an event is being encoded, the schema chosen to organize that encoding must be selected according to the one that best fits the event: it would be no good encoding a picnic with a schema for going to the office! So the event pattern must be matched with the best-fitting schema pattern.

SAQ 17
For unit Y, the input activity 1 exceeds its threshold so it turns on (produces output activity value 1). For unit Z, the input activity 0 does not exceed its threshold, so it turns off (output activity 0). For unit X, the total input activity is $1 \times 1 = 1$ from unit Y, added to $1 \times 0 = 0$ from unit Z. The total of 1 is less than its threshold so it turns off (its output is 0).

SAQ 18
One set of associations would be: (00 with 0), (01, 10 and 11 with 1). All that is needed to store this set of associations is to change the threshold of unit X to 0.5. Another set of possible associations with different weights would be (00, 01 with 0), (10, 11 with 1).

SAQ 19

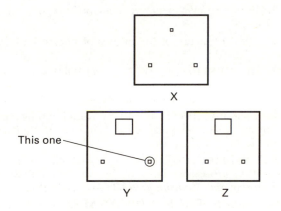

SAQ 20
The output to 01 would be 1. The output to 11 would be 2.

SAQ 21
It is found in the leftmost very large square in the top row, and is the only large square inside it. This means it has a strong, positive connection. The ceiling descriptor is not strongly asociated with any other descriptor.

SAQ 22
The units on after cueing with bathtub and ceiling are: scale, toilet, cupboard, sink, very small, door and walls (as well as the two cues bathtub and ceiling, of course). Unit 'cupboard' turns on late and appears not to reach full strength.

SAQ 23
The weights after the third presentation are: 0.525, 1.05, 0.237, 0.158, 0.6, 0.2.

SAQ 24
Spontaneous generalization. The network has generalized spontaneously across all the correlated stimuli to form a composite response.

References

ALBA, J.W. and HASHER, L. (1983) 'Is memory schematic?', *Psychological Bulletin*, 93, pp. 203–31.

ALLPORT, D.A. (1980) 'Attention and performance', in G. Glaxton (ed.) *Cognitive Psychology: New Directions*, Routledge and Kegan Paul.

ANDERSON, J. (1973) 'A theory for the recognition of items from short memorized lists', *Psychological Review*, 80, pp. 417–38.

ANDERSON, J. (1976) *Language, Memory and Thought.*, Erlbaum.

ANDERSON, J. (1983) *The Architecture of Cognition*, Harvard University Press.

ANDERSON, J. (1989a) 'Human memory: an adaptive perspective', *Psychological Review*, 96, pp. 703–19.

ANDERSON, J. (1989b) 'Theory of the origins of human knowledge', *Artificial Intelligence*, 40, pp. 313–51.

ANDERSON, J., SILVERSTEIN, J., RITZ, S. and JONES, R. (1977) 'Distinctive features, categorical perception, and probability learning: some applications of a neural model', *Psychological Review*, 84, pp. 413–51.

ANDERSON, R.C. and PICHERT, J.W. (1978) 'Recall of previously unrecallable information following a shift in perspective', *Journal of Verbal Learning and Verbal Behavior*, 17, pp. 1–12.

ATKINSON, R.C. and SHIFFRIN, R.M. (1968) 'Human memory: a proposed system and its control processes', in K.W. Spence and J.T. Spence (eds) *The Psychology of Learning and Motivation*, vol.2, Academic Press.

ATKINSON, R.C. and SHIFFRIN, R.M. (1971) 'The control of short-term memory', *Scientific American*, 225, pp. 82–90.

BADDELEY, A.D. (1968) 'A three-minute reasoning test based on grammatical transformation', *Psychonomic Science*, 10, pp. 341–2.

BADDELEY, A.D. (1979) 'Working memory and reading', in P.A. Kolers, M.E. Wrolstad, and H. Bouma (eds) *Processing of Visible Language*, Plenum.

BADDELEY, A.D. (1981a) 'The concept of working memory: a view of its current state and probable future development', *Cognition*, 10, pp. 17–23.

BADDELEY, A.D. (1981b) 'Reading and working memory', *Bulletin of the British Psychological Society*, 35, pp. 414–17.

BADDELEY, A.D. (1990) *Human Memory: Theory and Practice*, Lawrence Erlbaum Associates.

BADDELEY, A.D. (1992) 'Is working memory working?', The Fifteenth Bartlett Lecture, *Quarterly Journal of Experimental Psychology*, 44A, pp. 1–31.

BADDELEY, A.D., ELDRIDGE, M. and LEWIS, V.J. (1981) 'The role of subvocalisation in reading', *Quarterly Journal of Experimental Psychology*, 33a, pp. 439–54.

BADDELEY, A.D. and HITCH, G. (1974) 'Working memory', in G.H. Bower (ed.) *The Psychology of Learning and Motivation*, vol.8, Academic Press.

BADDELEY, A.D. and LIEBERMAN, K. (1980) 'Spatial working memory', in R.S. Nickerson (ed.) *Attention and Performance*, vol.VIII, Erlbaum.

BADDELEY, A.D., THOMSON, N. and BUCHANAN, M. (1975) 'Word length and the structure of short-term memory', *Journal of Verbal Learning and Verbal Behavior*, 14, pp. 575–89.

BANAJI, M.R. and CROWDER, R.G. (1989) 'The bankruptcy of everyday memory', *American Psychologist*, 44, pp. 1185–93.

BARTLETT, F.C. (1932) *Remembering*, Cambridge University Press.

BECHTEL, W. and ABRAHAMSEN, A. (1991) *Connectionism and the Mind: An Introduction to Parallel Processing in Networks*, Basil Blackwell.

BREWER, W.F. and TREYENS, J.C. (1981) 'Role of schemata in memory for places', *Cognitive Psychology*, 13, pp. 207–30.

BROADBENT, D.E., COOPER, P.F., FITZGERALD, P. and PARKES, K.R. (1982) 'The cognitive failures questionnaire (CFQ) and its correlates', *British Journal of Clinical Psychology*, 21, pp. 1–18.

BROWN, G.D.A. (1987) 'Resolving inconsistency: a computational model of word naming', *Journal of Memory and Language*, 26, pp. 1–2.

BROWN, R. and KULIK, J. (1982) 'Flashbulb memory', in U. Neisser (ed.) *Memory Observed*, W.H. Freeman.

COHEN, G. (1989) *Memory in the Real World*, Erlbaum.

COHEN, G. (1990) 'Memory', in Roth, I. (ed.) *Introduction to Psychology: Volume 2*, Lawrence Erlbaum Associates and The Open University.

COHEN, G. and FAULKNER, D. (1984) 'Everyday memory in the over-sixties', *New Scientist*, October.

CONWAY, M. (1990) *Autobiographical Memory: An Introduction*, Open University Press.

CRICK, F. and ASANUMA, C. (1986) 'Certain aspects of the anatomy and physiology of the cerebral cortex', in J.L. McClelland, D.E. Rumelhart and the PDP Research Group (eds) *Parallel Distributed Processing: Explorations in the Microstructure of Cognition, Vol.2, Psychological and Biological Models*, MIT Press/Bradford Books.

ELLIS, A.W. (1993) *Reading, Writing and Dyslescia* (2nd edn.), Lawrence Erlbaum Associates.

EYSENCK, M.W. and KEANE, M. (1990) *Cognitive Psychology: A Student's Handbook*, Lawrence Erlbaum Associates.

FODOR, J.A. (1983) *The Modularity of Mind*, MIT Press.

FODOR, J.A. and PYLYSHYN, Z.W. (1988) 'Connectionism and cognitive architecture: a critical analysis', *Cognition*, 28, pp. 3–71.

GEISELMAN, R.E., FISHER, R.P., MACKINNON, D.P. and HOLLAND, H.L. (1985) 'Eyewitness memory enhancement in the police interview', *Journal of Applied Psychology*, 70, pp. 401–12.

GRAESSER, A.C. and NAKAMURA, G.V. (1982) 'The impact of a schema on comprehension and memory', in G.H. Bower (ed.) *The Psychology of Learning and Motivation: Advances in Research and Theory*, Academic Press.

HANSON, S.J. and BURR, D.J. (1990) 'What connectionist models learn: learning and representation in connectionist networks', *Behavioural and Brain Sciences*, 13, pp. 471–518.

References

HARDYCK, C.D. and PETRINOVICH, L.F. (1970) 'Subvocal speech and comprehension levels as a function of the difficulty level of reading material', *Journal of Verbal Learning and Verbal Behavior*, 9, pp. 647–52.

HARRIS, R.J. (1978) 'The effects of jury size and judge's instructions on memory for pragmatic implications from courtroom testimony', *Bulletin of the Psychonomic Society*, 11, pp. 129–32.

HARRIS, R.J. and MONACO, G.E. (1976) 'Psychology of pragmatic implication: information processing between the lines', *Journal of Experimental Psychology: General*, 107, pp. 1–22.

HINTON, G.E. and SEJNOWSKI, T.J. (1986) 'Learning and relearning in Boltzmann Machines', in J.L. McClelland, D.E. Rumelhart and the PDP Research Group (eds) *Parallel Distributed Processing: Explorations in the Microstructure of Cognition, Vol.1, Foundations*, MIT Press/Bradford Books.

HINTZMAN, D.L. (1986) 'Schema abstraction in a multiple-trace memory model', *Psychological Review*, 93, pp. 411–28.

HITCH, G. and BADDELEY, A.D. (1976) 'Verbal reasoning and working memory', *Quarterly Journal of Experimental Psychology*, 28, pp. 603–21.

HOLDING, D.H., NOONAN, T.K., PFAU, H.D. and HOLDING, C.S. (1986) 'Date attribution, age, and the distribution of lifetime memories', *Journal of Gerontology*, 41, pp. 481–5.

HUBEL, D.H. and WIESEL, T.N. (1959) 'Receptive fields of single neurones in the cat's striate cortex', *Journal of Physiology*, 148, pp. 574–91.

HUBEL, D.H. and WIESEL, T.N. (1962) 'Receptive fields, binocular interaction and functional architecture in the cat's visual cortex', *Journal of Physiology*, 16, pp. 106–54.

HUEY, E.B. (1908) *The Psychology and Pedagogy of Reading*, Macmillan.

HULICKA, I.M. (1982) 'Memory functioning in late adulthood', in F.I.M. Craik and S. Trehub (eds) *Advances in the Study of Communication and Affect, Vol. 8: Aging and Cognitive Processes*, Plenum Press.

HUNT, E. (1980) 'Intelligence as an information-processing concept', *British Journal of Psychology*, 71, pp. 449–77.

JAMES, W. (1899) *Talks to Teachers on Psychology, and to Students on Some of Life's Ideals*, Holt.

KLIEGL, R. and BALTES, P.B. (1987) 'Theory guided analysis of developing and aging mechanisms through testing-the-limits and research on expertise', in C. Schooler and K.W. Schaie (eds) *Cognitive Functioning and Social Structure over the Life Course*, Norwood, N.J., Ablex.

KUCERA, H. and FRANCIS, W.N. (1967) 'Computational analysis of present-day American English', *Providence*, RI: Brown University Press.

KURODA, S.Y. (1987) 'Where is Chomsky's bottleneck?', *Centre for Research in Language Newsletter* (University of California, San Diego), 1, pp. 4–11.

LABERGE, D. (1981) 'Automatic information processing: a review', in J. Long and A. Baddeley (eds) *Attention and Performance*, vol.IX, Erlbaum.

LACHMANN, J.L., LACHMAN, R. and THRONESBERRY, C. (1979) 'Metamemory through the adult life span', *Developmental Psychology*, 15, pp. 543–51.

LAIRD, J.E., NEWELL, A. and ROSENBLOOM, P.S. (1987) 'SOAR: an architecture for general intelligence', *Artificial Intelligence*, 33, pp. 1–64.

LENAT, D.B. (1977) 'Automated theory formation in mathematics', in *Proceedings of the Fifth International Joint Conference on Artificial Intelligence*, MIT, Cambridge, MA, pp. 833–42.

LEVY, B.A. (1978) 'Speech processing during reading', in A.M. Lesgold, J.W. Pellegrino, S.D. Fokkema, and R. Glaser (eds) *Cognitive Psychology and Instruction*, Plenum.

LINTON, M. (1982) 'Transformation of memory in everyday life', in U. Neisser (ed.) *Memory Observed*, W.H. Freeman.

LIST, J.A. (1986) 'Age and schematic differences in the reliability of eyewitness testimony', *Developmental Psychology*, 22, pp. 50–7.

LOFTUS, E.F. (1975) 'Leading questions and the eye-witness report', *Cognitive Psychology*, 7, pp. 560–72.

LOFTUS, E.F. (1979) 'Reactions to blatantly contradictory information', *Memory and Cognition*, 7, pp. 368–74.

LOFTUS, E.F., MILLER, D.G. and BURNS, H.J. (1978) 'Semantic integration of verbal information into a visual memory', *Journal of Experimental Psychology, Human Learning and Memory*, 4, pp. 19–31.

McCLELLAND, J.L. and RUMELHART, D.E. (1986) 'A distributed model of human learning and memory', in J.L. McClelland, D.E. Rumelhart and the PDP Research Group (eds) *Parallel Distributed Processing: Explorations in the Microstructure of Cognition, Vol.2, Psychological and Biological Models*, MIT Press/ Bradford Books.

McKOON, A., RATCLIFF, R. and DELL, G.S. (1986) 'A critical evaluation of the semantic-episodic distinction', *Journal of Experimental Psychology: Learning, Memory and Cognition*, 12, pp. 295–306.

MEDIN, D.L. and SCHAFFER, M.M. (1978) 'Context theory of classification learning', *Psychological Review*, 85, pp. 207–38.

MILLER, G.A. (1956) 'The magical number seven plus or minus two', *Psychological Review*, 63, pp. 81–97.

MORRIS, R. (ed.) (1989) *Parallel Distributed Processing*, Oxford University Press.

NEISSER, U. (1978) 'Memory: what are the important questions?', in M.M. Gruneberg, P.E. Morris and R.N. Sykes (eds) *Practical Aspects of Memory*, Academic Press.

NEISSER, U. (1982) *Memory Observed*, W.H. Freeman.

NELSON, K. (1986) *Event Knowledge: Structure and Function in Development*, Lawrence Erlbaum Associates.

NEWELL, A. (1973) 'Production systems: models of control structures', in W. Chase (ed.) *Visual Information Processing*, Academic Press.

NEWELL, A. (1989) *Unified Theories of Cognition*, Harvard University Press.

NORMAN, D.A. (1981) 'Categorization of action slips', *Psychological Review*, 88, pp. 1–15.

NORMAN, D.A. and BOBROW, D.G. (1979) 'Descriptions: an intermediate stage in memory retrieval', *Cognitive Psychology*, 11, pp. 107–23.

References

NORMAN, D.A. and SHALLICE, T. (1980) *Attention to Action: Willed and Automatic Control of Behavior*, University of California, San Diego, CHIP Report 99.

PETERSON, L.R. and PETERSON, M.J. (1959) 'Short-term retention of individual items', *Journal of Experimental Psychology*, 58, pp. 193–8.

POLLACK, J.B. (1990) 'Recursive distributed representations', *Artificial Intelligence*, 46, pp. 77–105.

RAYNER, K., CARLSON, M. and FRAZIER, L. (1983) 'The interaction of syntax and semantics during sentence processing: eye movements in the analysis of semantically biased sentences', *Journal of Verbal Learning and Verbal Behavior*, 22, pp. 358–74.

REASON, J.T. (1979) 'Actions not as planned: the price of automatization', in G. Underwood and R. Stevens (eds) *Aspects of Consciousness*, vol.1, Academic Press.

RICHARDSON, J.T.E. (1984) 'Developing the theory of working memory', *Memory and Cognition*, 12, pp. 71–83.

ROSCH, E. (1978) 'Principles of categorisation', in E. Rosch and B.B. Lloyd (eds) *Cognition and Categorisation*, Lawrence Erlbaum Associates.

ROTH, I. (ed.) (1990) *Introduction to Psychology, Volume 2*, Lawrence Erlbaum Associates in association with The Open University.

RUBIN, D.C. and KOZIN, M. (1984) 'Vivid memories', *Cognition*, 16, pp. 81–5.

RUMELHART, D.E., HINTON, G.E. and McCLELLAND, J.L. (1986) 'A general framework for parallel distributed processing', in J.L. McClelland, D.E. Rumelhart and the PDP Research Group (eds) *Parallel Distributed Processing: Explanations in the Microstructure of Cognition, Vol.1, Foundations*, MIT Press/ Bradford Books.

RUMELHART, D.E. and McCLELLAND (1986) 'On learning the past tense of English verbs', in J.L. McClelland, D.E. Rumelhart and the PDP Research Group (eds) *Parallel Distributed Processing: Explorations in the Microstructure of Cognition, Vol.2, Psychological and Biological Models*, MIT Press/Bradford Books.

RUMELHART, D.E. and NORMAN, D.A. (1983) 'Representation in memory', in R.C. Atkinson, R.J. Herrnstein, G. Lindzey and R.D Luce (eds) *Handbook of Experimental Psychology*, Wiley and Sons.

RUMELHART, D.E., SMOLENSKY, P., McCLELLAND, J.L. and HINTON, G.E. (1986) 'Schematic and sequential thought processes in PDP Models', in J.L. McClelland, D.E. Rumelhart and the PDP Research Group (eds) *Parallel Distributed Processing: Explorations in the Microstructure of Cognition, Vol.2, Psychological and Biological Models*, MIT Press/Bradford Books.

SCHANK, R. (1981) 'Language and memory', in D.A. Norman (ed.) *Perspectives on Cognitive Sciences*, Erlbaum.

SEIDENBERG, M.S. and McCLELLAND, J.L. (1989) 'A distributed, developmental model of word recognition and naming', *Psychological Review*, 96, pp. 523–68.

SIMON, H. (1974) 'How big is a chunk?', *Science*, 183, pp. 482–8.

SMOLENSKY, P. (1986) 'Neural and conceptual interpretation of PDP models', in J.L. McClelland, D.E. Rumelhart and the PDP Research Group (eds) *Parallel Distributed Processing: Explorations in the Microstructure of Cognition, Vol.2, Psychological and Biological Models*, MIT Press/Bradford Books.

SMOLENSKY, P. (1988) 'On the proper treatment of connectionism', *Behavioural and Brain Sciences*, 11, pp. 1–74.

SUNDERLAND, A., HARRIS, J.E. and BADDELEY, A.D. (1983) 'Do laboratory tests predict everyday memory? A neuropsychological study', *Journal of Verbal Learning and Verbal Behavior*, 22, pp. 341–57.

TARABAN, R. and McCLELLAND, J.L. (1987) 'Conspiracy effects in word recognition', *Journal of Memory and Language*, 26, pp. 608–31.

TULVING, E. (1972) 'Episodic and semantic memory', in E. Tulving and W. Donaldson (eds) *Organization of Memory*, Academic Press.

TULVING, E. (1984) 'How many memory systems are there?', Address to the American Psychological Association, reprinted in *American Psychologist* (1985), 40, pp. 385–98.

TULVING, E. (1991) 'Memory research is not a zero-sum game', *American Psychologist*, 46, pp. 41–2.

VALLACHER, R.R. and WEGNER, D.M. (1987) 'What do people think they're doing? Action identification and human behaviour', *Psychological Review*, 94, pp. 3–15.

WAGENAAR, W.A. (1986) 'My memory: a study of autiobiographical memory over six years', *Cognitive Psychology*, 18, pp. 225–52.

WATERS, G.S. and SEIDENBERG, M.S. (1985) 'Spelling-sound effects in reading: time course and decision criteria', *Memory and Cognition*, 13, pp. 557–72.

WHITE, P. (1988) 'Knowing more about what we can tell: "introspective access" and causal report accuracy 10 years later', *British Journal of Psychology*, 79, pp. 13–45.

WHITTEN, W.B. and LEONARD, J.M. (1981) 'Directed search through autobiographical memory', *Memory and Cognition*, 9, pp. 566–79.

WICKELGREN, W.A. (1969) 'Context-sensitive coding, associative memory, and serial order in (speech) behaviour', *Psychological Review*, 76, pp. 1–15.

WILDING, J. and MOHINDRA, D. (1980) 'Effects of subvocal suppression, articulating aloud and noise on sequence', *British Journal of Psychology*, 71, pp. 247–61.

WILKINS, A.J. (1976) 'A failure to demonstrate the effects of retention interval', cited in J.E. Harris, 'Remembering to do things: a forgotten topic', in J.E. Harris and P.E. Morris (eds) *Everyday Actions and Absentmindedness*, Academic Press.

WILLIAMS, M.D. and HOLLAN, J.D. (1981) 'The process of retrieval from very long term memory', *Cognitive Science*, 5, pp. 87–119.

Index of Authors

Index of Authors

Laird, J.E., Newell, A. and
  Rosenbloom, P.S. (1987)   94
Lenat, D.B. (1977)   171
Levy, B.A. (1978)   86
Linton, M. (1982)   52–3
List, J.A. (1986)   39
Loftus, E.F. (1975)   35–6
Loftus, E.F. (1979)   38, 41
Loftus, E.F., Miller, D.G. and Burns,
  H.J. (1978)   36–7

McClelland, J.L. and Rumelhart, D.E.
  (1986)   147–54
McKoon, A., Ratcliff, R. and Dell,
  G.S. (1986)   51
Medin, D.L. and Schaffer, M.M.
  (1978)   148
Miller, G.A. (1956)   19, 68
Morris, R. (ed.) (1989)   173

Neisser, U. (1978)   15
Neisser, U. (1982)   56
Nelson, K. (1986)   32
Newell, A. (1973)   94, 112
Newell, A. (1989)   94
Norman, D.A. (1981)   46
Norman, D.A., and Bobrow, D.G.
  (1979)   58–9
Norman, D.A. and Shallice, T. (1980)
  79

Peterson, L.R. and Peterson, M.J.
  (1959)   15–16
Pollack, J.B. (1990)   170

Rayner, K., Carlson, M. and
  Frazier, L. (1983)   87
Reason, J.T. (1979)   44
Richardson, J.T.E. (1984)   88–9
Rosch, E. (1978)   148
Roth, I. (ed.) (1990)   90

Rubin, D.C. and Kozin, M. (1984)
  56
Rumelhart, D.E., Hinton, G.E. and
  McClelland, J.L. (1986)   157
Rumelhart, D.E. and McClelland, J.L.
  (1986)   159
Rumelhart, D.E. and Norman, D.A.
  (1983)   28–9
Rumelhart, D.E., Smolensky, P.,
  McClelland, J.L. and Hinton, G.E.
  (1986)   131–8

Schank, R.C. (1981)   35
Seidenberg, M.S. and McClelland, J.L.
  (1989)   159–65
Simon, H. (1974)   68–9
Smolensky, P. (1986)   166
Smolensky, P. (1988)   117
Sunderland, A., Harris, J.E. and
  Baddeley, A.D. (1983)   22

Taraban, R. and McClelland, J.L.
  (1987)   160, 161
Tulving, E. (1972)   50
Tulving, E. (1984)   50
Tulving, E. (1991)   120

Vallacher, R.R. and Wegner, D.M.
  (1987)   47

Wagenaar, W.A. (1986)   55
Waters, G.S. and Seidenberg, M.S.
  (1985)   161, 162
White, P. (1988)   19
Whitten, W.B. and Leonard, J.M.
  (1981)   57
Wickelgren, W.A. (1969)   159
Wilding, J. and Mohindra, N. (1980)
  74–5
Wilkins, A.J. (1976)   49
Williams, M.D. and Hollan, J.D.
  (1981)   57–8

Index of Concepts

Index of Concepts